GOLF'S THREE NOBLE TRUTHS

GOLF'S THREE NOBLE TRUTHS

THE FINE ART OF PLAYING AWAKE

JAMES RAGONNET

New World Library
Novato, California

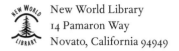

New World Library
14 Pamaron Way
Novato, California 94949

Copyright © 2007 by James Ragonnet

All rights reserved. This book may not be reproduced in whole or in part, stored in a retrieval system, or transmitted in any form or by any means — electronic, mechanical, or other — without written permission from the publisher, except by a reviewer, who may quote brief passages in a review.

Text design by Mary Ann Casler
Typography by Tona Pearce Myers

Library of Congress Cataloging-in-Publication Data
Ragonnet, James, 1944–
  Golf's three noble truths : the fine art of playing awake / James Ragonnet.
    p.   cm.
ISBN 978-1-57731-580-3 (hardcover : alk. paper)
1. Golf—Miscellanea. 2. Golf—Humor. I. Title.
GV967.R315 2007
796.352—dc22   2006103017

First printing, April 2007
ISBN-10: 1-57731-580-4
ISBN-13: 978-1-57731-580-3

Printed in Canada on acid-free, partially recycled paper

g New World Library is a proud member of the Green Press Initiative.

10 9 8 7 6 5 4 3 2 1

Especially for
Jamie

CONTENTS

"Hell is truth seen too late."

—— WILLIAM SLOAN COFFIN

"Growth is the only evidence of life."

—— CARDINAL JOHN HENRY NEWMAN

*"The simplest and most necessary truths are
always the last believed."*

—— JOHN RUSKIN

*"If you bring forth what is within you,
what you bring forth will save you.
If you do not bring forth what is within you,
what you do not bring forth will destroy you."*

—— THE GOSPEL OF THOMAS

*"Happiness is neither virtue nor pleasure, nor this nor that,
but simply growth. We are happy when we are growing."*

—— W. B. YEATS

INTRODUCTION

I have been playing golf for forty years — since I was twelve. For the first three decades, I wandered the fairways aimlessly, searching for fulfillment and inner satisfaction. But I was far from attaining what all golfers seek — whether they admit it or not — namely, a deep and permanent sense of "Ah, yes, this is what golf was meant to be."

My golf seeds, the ones I planted when I was twelve, weren't flowering into what they were meant to become.

When you plant seeds, you expect them to grow into healthy plants. Well, that didn't happen to my seeds. I didn't grow as a golfer. Despite some occasional buds and a few fruits — some low scores and a trophy here and there — I experienced what I consider minimal growth, even though I tried everything to get those meager buds and fruits to grow.

Before I got the idea for this book ten years ago, I felt empty. I sensed that something was missing. I wasn't missing only the external things — longer drives, lower scores, new graphite irons. All golfers miss those external things. I was also missing internal things — bliss, contentment, inner satisfaction, and peace of mind.

I kept hearing a whisper inside my head: "This isn't what golf is supposed to be." That whisper lasted until I woke up.

Awakened, I finally decided to take a new approach. I stopped focusing on the buds and fruits — the external things. And I started focusing on my roots — the internal things. That's when I started to learn and grow. That's also when I found my bliss. Bliss does not flow from external things. Bliss is a by-product of learning and growth.

When you examine your roots, you'll discover your core truths. You need to stop everything and look inside deeply and honestly. That's just what the Buddha did. After wandering around for seven years searching for enlightenment, he got fed up. He said to himself, "Okay, that's it!"

That night he sat under a fig tree and vowed not to move until he attained enlightenment. Facing east, he sat alone in the moonlight and looked into his core. By morning, he had attained enlightenment. He then announced his "Four Noble Truths."

By *noble* he meant worthy or highly ethical — not aristocratic. The Buddha used *noble* to denote one path of enlightenment for all people — not one path for the highborn and another for the lowly.

After years of wandering aimlessly, I finally stopped and looked inside myself. Having studied Eastern precepts and practices for some time, I naturally (though belatedly) turned to the East for inspiration. I stilled my mind and went within. Ten years later I found what I was looking for — my Three Noble Truths. What took the Buddha one night, took me a decade!

When the Buddha attained enlightenment, he shared his Four Noble Truths with a few close friends. Then, in a famous sermon delivered near the town of Benares, the Buddha publicly explained his Four Noble Truths for the first time. And so too with me. This book is *my* "Sermon at Benares."

When you're willing to face the truth — after stumbling and fumbling along — you'll find out who you are. When you get tired of looking outside, you'll turn within. Your truths, like oil deposits under layers of shale, reside deep within. If you drill deeply enough, you'll find them.

Truths give meaning and harmony to your life. Without core truths, you'll remain dull and asleep. That's the way I was!

This book is an invitation to consider certain truths. Perhaps these truths will spur your growth as they did mine. I can share these truths and invite you to grow. However, growth is a gift you must give to yourself.

Like the Buddha, I describe my truths as "noble." I respectfully suggest *one* worthy path for all golfers — the highborn and lowborn alike. Along my golf journey, Dear Golfer, these are the Three Noble Truths that I discovered.

THE FIRST NOBLE TRUTH: AWARENESS

Most likely, you're asleep and don't know it. If you're asleep, as I was, it's time to wake up, open your eyes, and pay attention to what's going on inside and outside yourself. All golf buddhas — Bobby Jones, Jack Nicklaus, Annika Sörenstam, Tiger Woods — play with their outer and inner eyes wide open.

All learning, growth, fulfillment, and bliss boil down to only one thing: *awareness*. Infuse every observation, motion, gesture, action, strategy, method, technique, routine, and breath with awareness. Let awareness well up and bubble over inside you. You're alive and kicking in proportion to your level of awareness.

THE SECOND NOBLE TRUTH: BALANCE

Establish your equilibrium, maintain your center, and avoid the extremes. When you're in balance, you're loose, clearheaded, and relaxed. Out of balance, you're constrained, confused, and tense.

Don't think too much or too little. Or swing too quickly or too slowly, adopt too flat or too upright a swing plane, grip too firmly or too loosely, get too elated or too depressed, expend too much or too little energy, have too much or too little confidence. Stay in the middle, and you'll stay out of trouble.

THE THIRD NOBLE TRUTH: UNITY

Outside and inside are false divisions. There are no divisions. Start uniting and seeing everything as one. A golf ball's cover, for example, is convex on the outside and concave on the inside. There's no separate inside and outside. Both sides form one cover. Everything is one, including you.

Find ways to unite everything around you. The more successfully you unite things — mind and body, head and heart, you and your playing partners, club and ball, you and the course — the more you'll learn, grow, and enjoy. Most important, when you start uniting things, you'll be surprised at how much delightful stuff you've been missing out on.

Recently, these Three Noble Truths crystallized into one dramatic experience. (You might say I had an OOGE — an "out-of-golf-experience.")

One sunny summer morning, I stood on the twelfth green lining up a ten-foot birdie putt. Having bogeyed the previous two holes, I dearly wanted to sink the putt. I surveyed the line from different angles, examined the slope of the green, observed the grain. Here's what I was looking at: a slightly downhill, down-grain putt with a subtle left-to-right break on a slow green that hadn't been cut yet. I moved energy from my heart to my head to nail this birdie.

I didn't want to stroke the putt too firmly and run the ball several feet past the cup, leaving myself a tester for par. I recalled the putts I had missed on the past two holes. I didn't want to repeat the same mistakes.

To drain this putt, I had to be aware of everything. I had to visualize the line, relax my hands, steady my head, keep my left eye over the ball, use a short takeaway, accelerate slightly on my follow-through, start the stroke with my left shoulder, and hope for the best.

That's when it happened! A butterfly landed on my shoe. It was too good to be true. A beautiful lemon-yellow butterfly — wings outlined in black — sat motionless on the toe of my saddle shoe. I shifted my energy from my head to my heart. From the realm of rationality, I was suddenly in the realm of emotionality.

Transfixed and enthralled, I marveled at the delicate creature on my shoe. Nothing mattered more than this butterfly. It was a sacramental moment. An inexpressible and unfathomable feeling of awe and mystery enveloped me. Time stood still.

I was in the presence of something unearthly. My focus shifted from the putt to the butterfly. A moment before I had been observing the mundane. Now I was glimpsing the mystical. The butterfly — a blessing, a benediction, a grace — appeared from nowhere.

The butterfly's presence awakened me to a whole new order. This winged messenger reminded me to wake up, to cherish fleeting and precious things, to stop taking things for granted, to treasure the sublime. A moment ago, I had focused on my putt — on actualizing my *doing*. Now I focused on the butterfly — on actualizing my *being*.

When the butterfly flew away, I returned to my putt. However, everything seemed different. Before I had felt needy, apprehensive, and incomplete. Now I felt fulfilled, calm, and whole. I felt totally centered, balanced, and refreshed.

I doubt if anyone else in my foursome even saw the butterfly. They were fixated on their putting. Frankly, that's what made the moment so special. That precious yellow butterfly belonged exclusively to me.

The First Noble Truth — awareness — was dramatically illustrated on the twelfth green. I opened my awareness to both birdie putt and yellow butterfly. Both represented precious opportunities for growth. Total growth — fulfilling your golf potential and your human potential — means capitalizing on the finite number of birdie and butterfly opportunities you're afforded.

Golf's reward is not what you *get* but what you *become*. Moment to moment, you're infinitely rich or immensely poor, depending on your level of awareness.

The Second Noble Truth — balance — was also manifest during this precious moment. When the butterfly landed on my shoe, a wave of contentment rolled over me. Totally at ease, I became acutely aware of everything happening around me. I remained calm and centered as I absorbed the butterfly's magical presence and glimpsed its mystery. Only that moment mattered.

Everything — the blue sky, the tall pines, the birds singing, the green fairway — became very serene. I didn't go to intellectual or emotional extremes. I didn't try to name or classify the butterfly, or estimate the size of its wings, or think about what butterflies ate, or figure out where this butterfly had come from. I avoided the extremes and stayed in the middle.

The Third Noble Truth — unity — also manifested itself in this moment. If I had ignored the butterfly and focused on my putt, I would have missed an opportunity to *be* more. However, if I had ignored the putt and focused only on the butterfly, I would have missed an opportunity to *do* more. By focusing on both, I actualized total growth. Golf was all about the butterfly. And the butterfly was all about golf.

During that magical and ecstatic moment, the butterfly and I merged. This unified encounter provided me with a blissful and poignant reminder that golf has ten thousand doors. However, only in a state of *awareness*, *balance*, and *unity* can you open those doors.

Bringing awareness, balance, and unity to your game is like bringing a fresh supply of blood to a nagging injury like a sprained ankle or torn muscle. Without a fresh and continuous supply of blood to the area of your injury, it won't heal and the pain won't go away. That's why golfers with sprains and muscle tears use physical therapy.

The same holds true for your ailing golf game. This book — containing therapeutic insights, methods, and techniques — is designed to circulate a rich, fresh, and continuous supply of awareness, balance, and unity into your game. That's the only way you'll recover and make your pain go away. The therapeutic lessons here resemble Eastern art forms — like Japanese poems or paintings — that juxtapose simple truths to impart flashes of understanding.

They are arranged randomly. Knowledge and logic are orderly and arranged. Wisdom and intuition, however — like yellow butterflies resting on your shoe — are random and unexpected.

Eastern thinkers say you have two birthdays. Your First Birthday is the day you emerge from your mother's womb. Your

Second Birthday is the day you wake up to everything happening around you.

This book celebrates my Second Birthday. That's when the birdies started to show up, when my handicap started to drop, when I started to laugh at myself, when I started to appreciate the deep blue sky, when I started to grow totally... and when inner bliss — like winged monarch butterflies — started fluttering inside me.

DEAD PEOPLE DON'T PLAY GOLF

After you're gone, Dear Golfer, who'll ever walk down the fairway the way you do? Duck-hook a drive into the woods the way you do? Listen at dusk to the mourning doves the way you do? Drive a golf cart the way you do? Pull the flagstick from the cup the way you do? Throw a golf bag in the back of a pickup truck the way you do? Line up a putt the way you do? Who will ever (except Jacques perhaps) shank a ball the way you do? (Geez Louise, you ought to see my friend Jacques shank a ball!)

The answer is simple: nobody! Sure, others may try to imitate you. But no one can impersonate *you*. When you're gone, the way you do things will disappear. In this life you're granted a finite number of breaths, days, divots, and rounds of golf. Despite your illusions, life doesn't go on forever. Until you realize that, you're missing the whole point. You don't need a whole new golf life. You just need to cherish the golf life you already have.

Death isn't some enemy waiting to destroy you. Rather, death is a friend reminding you to drop your pretensions and pay attention. Death will whisper to you about your unfinished business. Whether you listen to what death is telling you — that's up to you. I don't know much, but I know this: That if I don't cherish the moments I have left, someday I'm going to regret it. Before death hunts me down, I'm going to bow more reverently to golf — even if I don't know what I'm bowing to.

Death may seem like an odd subject for a book on golf. But when the idea of cherishing life's precious moments arises, death is the only place to start. Why? Because death compels you to decide what really matters in your life. To understand the preciousness of life, just contemplate death. It's like an approaching flood or hurricane threatening to demolish your house. Before you flee the area, you must decide what to take with you. "All human beings," wrote James Thurber, "should try to learn before they die what they are running from, and to, and why."

Trophies and a big golf reputation certainly matter — but what matters far more is this: to find joy in a game you love with all your heart. When my heart's aglow and I'm enjoying a round of golf with some dear friends on a beautiful day, I've been known to proclaim, "If I could drop dead right now on this beautiful golf course, I'd be the happiest man alive!"

Learn to cherish golf's small miracles. The fairway bathed in green glory...the dew glistening on the fairway...the autumn trees clad in gleaming copper...the wind swirling the autumn leaves in the rough...the aroma of freshly mowed grass, the soft velvet of the green underfoot...the wispy pink clouds connecting afternoon to evening...the stroll toward your ball...the American flag standing tall by the deserted clubhouse at dusk.

The things you most cherish and think about make you the person you are. The things you place in the palace of your heart determine who you are. When you internalize golf's small miracles, *you* become the miracle. When you feel fully alive, fully awake, fully blessed — that's how you know you're standing in the right place. If you live joyfully, your life will never be a failure.

If you really want to come alive on the golf course, try this: imagine yourself lying dead in your fancy coffin. Picture a coffin large enough to accommodate you, your clubs, and that large Ping tour bag that Harold (your worthless, unemployed, ex-brother-in-law) sold you. Next, imagine yourself wearing your navy Cutter & Buck shirt, your Izod tan shorts, and your orange Niagara Falls CC golf hat. Imagine your lucky St. Andrews ball marker and divot tool in your pocket.

Imagine yourself, decked out as above, with your feet set in an open stance and your right shoulder positioned slightly lower than your left. Finally, picture your hands (in a Vardon grip) reverently folded across your chest. When you imagine yourself in your coffin, you'll get a whole new perspective. Suddenly, your golf problems won't seem that bad. (In fact, none of your problems will seem that bad.) This meditation exercise is a valuable reality check when things don't roll your way. Which is most of the time.

Consider each golf day a special gift. Slip each golf day — regardless of your score — into the archives where you store your most precious memories. When your golf moments are spent, they are lost forever. Eternity never gives them back. Before it's too late, acknowledge time's relentless melt. Don't wait until your final round to start loving golf. Don't wait until your last heartbeat to start loving life. Don't waste your last breath telling the EMT at your doorstep, "If anything should happen to me, please make sure George gets my new set of Mizuno irons."

Leo Tolstoy, the Russian novelist, said that the reality of death compels us to change our life in such a way as to give it a meaning that not even death can remove. From this instant forward, this is what's left of your life. So tell me, Dear Golfer, what do you plan to do with what remains of your precious golf life?

AWARENESS

Imagine yourself in a large conference room, along with one hundred other golfers taking a survey. The coordinator asks you to list the ten most vexing problems associated with your game. (You and other disgruntled golfers want to list more than ten, but the coordinator insists on the limit. You sense some hostility over this matter.)

Then the coordinator asks you to turn over the paper and list the ten most vexing problems associated with your health. After collecting the survey forms, the coordinator thanks the group for participating and invites everyone to return in a week to get the results. Before everyone leaves, however, the coordinator says, "Judging from the findings of previous surveys, you may be rather surprised at what I have to tell you next week." So you and the other golfers all agree to return.

A week goes by. The coordinator welcomes everyone back and summarizes the wide range of golf and health problems the survey revealed. He uses some colorful display charts to present his findings. You're surprised at the length of each list.

Next, the coordinator draws some basic conclusions. Based on the numerous golf and health problems cited in the survey, he bluntly reports, you and the others are definitely in the hurt locker. Apparently, this audience of golfers has plenty of problems!

The coordinator then asks what you would think if a physician promised everyone in the room — all one hundred golfers — *one* proven remedy for the dozens of health problems listed on the board. That's right — *one* remedy to cure everyone's pains, illnesses, ailments, and conditions. You marvel at the possibility of such an amazing remedy.

Now the coordinator confesses that he has some bad news and some good news. The bad news is that he can't offer one remedy to cure everyone's health problems. The good news, however, is that he can offer one remedy to cure everyone's golf problems. "Despite the nature and severity of your individual golf problems," he says, "there is one prescription, medicine, treatment, solution, remedy for your collective golf ills: *awareness*. Despite the complexity and diversity of your golf problems, awareness is the only medicine you need." He tells you that the way to improve your game dramatically (barring some physical or mental impairment) is simply to nourish your powers of awareness. If you want to improve your golf game, put awareness front and center!

Awareness is a liberating force that will tell you what matters most. You control *only* the things of which you're aware. The things of which you're not aware will ultimately control you. If you're unaware of the significance of things — like your grip or swing plane — then you're a prisoner to golf. If so, admit it. Liberate yourself by bringing awareness to the things around you. The greater your awareness, the fewer things will control and imprison you. If you want to become a self-sufficient golfer, sharpen your powers of awareness. Awareness — the key to growth — is your private path of guided discovery.

Your awareness, like money, is a finite resource. Let's say, for example, you have $100 of awareness at your disposal to spend on the green in order to make a critical ten-foot birdie putt. Accordingly, you spend $50 of awareness on the speed, grain, and break of the green and $50 of awareness on the requisite mind-body cues, such as softening your hands, keeping your head still, bringing the putter straight back, and accelerating through the stroke.

Having spent all your awareness money on those two big items, you have no awareness money left. You don't have $3 of awareness to spend observing what happened to Al's putt after it went by the hole. You don't have $2 of awareness to spend observing how spongy and wet the green feels underfoot. You don't even have $1 of awareness to spend removing a teeny pebble or granule in your line that will distort the roll.

To nourish your full awareness, learn to spend your "awareness cash" on as many things as possible, especially on little things. Learn to divide your awareness money on things both outside and inside you. Spend some awareness money on your thoughts and feelings, especially your confidence. Develop a checklist of how you want to spend your awareness money. Then set aside some spare awareness money for any last-minute things you may have overlooked.

Awareness means being conscious of what's happening at every moment. Being aware is synonymous with being watchful, alert, awake, mindful, attentive, observant, and perceptive. The opposite of being aware is being asleep, inattentive, oblivious, unobservant, and obtuse. Awareness will relax, center, and anchor you in the moment and intensify your sensibilities.

Being aware means being illuminated from within. When you become fully aware, the outside world stays the same. What changes is how you respond to the outside world. Once again, remember that your awareness is twofold. You must actively engage your hard awareness to actualize your intellectual center. And you must actively engage your soft awareness to actualize your heart center. Most golfers suffer from a poverty of awareness. They go about their business unaware of what's happening all around them. Without awareness, you'll make the same mistakes again and again. With awareness, however, you'll wake up, look deeply, and start to grow. Your golf problems — your short drives, weak irons, erratic putting, or negative thinking — will persist until you raise your level of awareness. Becoming aware means watching everything you do: your *actions*, your *thoughts*, your *feelings*, and your *watching*, itself.

First, watch your *actions* (and those of others). Become aware of every small movement and gesture. When you grip the club, watch how you position your hands. Watch how your partner grips the club and how she positions her hands. Watch your posture and the posture of others. Watch the position of your feet at address. Watch how far you bend at the waist and at the knees. Watch carefully the distance you stand from the ball. Watch how high you tee the ball. Watch the direction the flag blows on the green. Watch where your divots land. Watch how fast you remove your driver from your bag. Watch how quickly you walk or drive your cart. Watch how easily your partner swings her driver. Watch how your other partner overrotates his hips. Watch the puffy clouds moving lazily across the sky. Watch the wind-blown autumn leaves tumbling across the fairway. Watch the blue and pink ribbons of dusk vanish in the west.

Assuming you're somewhat athletic, the key difference between you and your favorite golf pro is essentially your respective levels of awareness. You may, in fact, be a more experienced golfer than your teaching pro. However, the pro has something you lack: awareness. Experience without awareness is meaningless. Unless you suffuse your golf experience with awareness, you're nothing but a sleepwalker on the course.

Greg Norman is a great example of someone with natural talent combined with keen awareness. At age fifteen, he could hit a ball 330 yards. At age twenty-one, he won the fourth pro tournament he ever entered. Obviously, being naturally athletic is important for a golfer. However, possessing awareness, especially self-awareness, is equally important. In sum, "Know thyself."

Second, watch your *thoughts*. Discriminate between important and unimportant thoughts. Keep discriminating among your thoughts as you play. Thoughts are like particles of dust on the mirror of your mind. The more dust that gathers on your mental mirror, the less clearly and accurately the mirror will reflect. Be watchful that not too much past-dust or future-dust gathers on your mental mirror. Watch for welcome gaps in your thoughts. Be watchful that your mind is not too cluttered.

Watch for indecisiveness. Watch your thoughts to decide exactly what you want to do. Watch your thoughts so you know exactly where you want to aim your putt — outside left edge, left edge, or in the middle. Watch your thoughts when you're unsure about what club to hit; which way a putt will break; what your yardage is to the creek; which way the wind is blowing; whether you want to lay up or go for it; or how far back to bring your putter to stroke a sixty-footer. Watch your thoughts for everything: confusion, contradictions, bravado, stubbornness, rigidity, narrowness, worry, anxiety, insights, and connections.

Third, watch your *emotions and physical sensations*. Pay attention to the feel of the clubhead as you swing. To the tension in your grip. To how much tension pervades your entire body. To how your rhythm and tempo feel. To whether your arms feel long and loose. To the feel of the ground as you establish a solid base. To whether you feel your shoulders rotating properly. To whether you feel your right shoulder on the downswing closing too early. To how soft your new putter grip is. To the cool, metallic feel of your 8-iron as you remove it from your bag. To what the wind feels like on your cheek. To what your anger and disappointment feel like when you miss an easy putt. Feel the anger and disappointment totally. Identify fully with both feelings. Then drop them.

Pay attention so that the anger and disappointment don't linger inside you. Don't deny the reality of the emotions. Just let them naturally pass like clouds or melt like snowflakes. Remain alert to all your feelings: the joy of draining a long putt, the agony of topping your fairway wood, the satisfaction of connecting your 7-iron squarely with the ball, the exasperation of seeing your chip shot roll twenty yards past the pin. Feel it all.

Finally, watch your *watching*. Become aware of your awareness. Golf — composed of innumerable small, subtle, and important things — demands that you play fully aware, fully awake, fully watchful. Watching your watchfulness occurs as long as you pay close attention to your actions, thoughts, and feelings. Awareness is a discipline and a practice, as well as a tendency and an inclination. Awareness is the only way to glimpse golf's hidden wholeness, to actualize your growth.

In the East, an enlightened person is someone totally aware, or completely awake. There is a famous story about what it means to be enlightened. A long time ago, a man traveled very far to visit a legendary Zen master whom he deeply admired. As the traveler neared the monastery, he approached an old man carrying water from his well. The traveler asked the old man, "Where can I find the master of this monastery?"

The old man chuckled and said, "I am the person you're looking for. I am the master of this monastery."

The traveler said, "I can't believe that you're the master. I never imagined you — of all people — carrying water and working like a menial servant."

The master replied, "But that's what I used to do before I became a master. Before I became enlightened, I carried water and chopped wood. Now I do exactly what I did before."

The traveler asked, "Then what's the difference in you? You're doing exactly the very same things that you did before you were enlightened. What's the point of being enlightened?"

The master laughed and said, "The difference is internal — not external. I do exactly the same things. What's different is *how* I do things. Before my enlightenment, I did everything mindlessly, as if I were asleep. Now I do everything fully alert, fully awake. That's the difference. I still carry water and chop wood. The difference is this: now I am awake. Therefore, I'm not the same person anymore. Since I'm not the same person anymore, carrying water and chopping wood also are not the same anymore."

To become awake is to become another person. Developing your awareness will sensitize you to the sublime and hidden elements of golf. For your golf game, there's only *one* prescription, medicine, treatment, solution, or remedy: awareness! You're alive in proportion to your degree of awareness. You're not alive just because you have brain waves, heartbeats, and breaths. Even gravely ill patients, right up to the end, have functioning brains, hearts, and lungs. You're alive in proportion to how awake you are.

In June 1930 Bobby Jones published an article in *The American Golfer* titled "The Hardest Thing in Golf." In his article Jones referred to Charles Lindbergh and his heroic solo flight of the *Spirit of St. Louis* across the Atlantic in 1927. Jones wrote, "Lindbergh said that the hardest thing he had to do in crossing the Atlantic was to keep awake. It is not so easy to understand why the hardest thing a golfer has to do is keep awake — mentally." In 1930 Jones won the British Open, British Amateur, U.S. Open, and U.S. Amateur — "The Grand Slam."

Who knows what staggering feats you are capable of if you learn to "stay awake." Like Charles Lindbergh and Bobby Jones, you might also receive a ticker-tape parade down Broadway's "Canyon of Heroes." Now wouldn't that be nice?

SPINNING YOUR WHEELS

You've just ended a nightmare round. Perhaps your worst round in ten years. You hit, at best, two good shots all day. In a light rain, you drive home feeling completely miserable. You're searching for one good reason not to commit suicide right after lunch. Mentally distracted and totally disgusted, you drive your monkey-shit-brown Honda into a muddy ditch. You think, "Oh, this is peachy! Now lunch and suicide will have to wait."

You try to drive out of the ditch. You back up — go forward — back up — go forward — back up — go forward. But you're hopelessly stuck. Your wheels just spin in the mud. From your glove compartment, you remove the handy leather-bound road-hazard manual that your mother-in-law gave you for your birthday. You read the part about getting out of ditches. You do exactly what the manual says. But it doesn't work. The wheels just continue to spin. (You can't wait to tell your know-it-all, condescending mother-in-law what you think about her road-hazard manual.)

Does spinning your wheels in a muddy ditch aptly characterize your golf game? You've read instructional books and watched videos, but no matter what you try, you just keep spinning your wheels. You've learned and tried a host of new and contradictory techniques drawn from golf magazines. But nothing has worked. You even took lessons from your club pro. However, as soon as he left, you again started to spin your wheels. Despite years of trying new stuff, *why* are you still stuck? And *how* do you get your game unstuck?

To stop spinning your wheels, start by learning more about *yourself.* Start by knowing that you don't know. What blocks growth is ignorance. What stimulates growth is awareness. When you're ignorant, you're unaware that you don't know. When you're enlightened, you're fully aware that you don't know.

For example, if you don't know that you're not gripping the club correctly, what's the use of toiling on the range to fix your swing plane? You're wasting your time. Sure, you need to correct your swing plane. But first you need to correct your grip. When you "don't know that you don't know," you're hammering cold iron.

"Knowing that you don't know" will give you the openness and freedom to target weaknesses and explore real options for growth. The worst golfers — those who exaggerate their abilities — possess the least amount of self-awareness. When you suffer from a lack of self-awareness, you remain in an information vacuum. Without self-awareness, you might as well be blind and deaf. "Not knowing that you don't know," you'll never grow.

Several years ago during a postgame press conference, a reporter asked Bill Parcells — then head coach of the New England Patriots football team — to comment on Drew Bledsoe's remarkable progress during his second season as a starting NFL quarterback. To explain Bledsoe's stunning improvement, Parcells said, "When you don't know that you *don't* know, it's a lot different than when you *do* know that you don't know. He [Bledsoe] knows now that he doesn't know. Last year, he didn't know that." In sum, when Bledsoe became aware that he didn't know, he began to improve.

One key to improving your game is learning how to manage your ego. If you don't manage your ego, you'll convince yourself that your game is fine. That's because your ego will lie to you. It will tell you exactly what you want to hear. Conversely, your humility — not your ego — will always tell you the truth. Your humility, if you listen to it, will tell you to change your grip, modify your stance, alter your posture, flatten your upright swing plane, or perhaps — scrap the whole mess and start over! Your humility will tell you what you *need* to hear, not what you *want* to hear.

If you're not inquisitive, if you think your swing is fine, you won't ask questions and look deeply. To stop spinning your wheels, ignore your ego and listen to your humility. Good golfers have keen internal radar, a honed self-awareness, that provides honest and accurate feedback. And that is the Breakfast of Champions.

Too often, a small taste of success will ruin you. Let's say you break 80 for the first time. Wow, are you pumped! To celebrate your career-best 79, you take that tightly folded, emergency twenty-dollar bill in your change purse to buy a round of drinks for your three playing partners. (Hopefully, your stingy husband never finds out about your impulsive display of largesse.)

You revel for weeks in the afterglow of that 79. Your ego keeps telling you how fantastic you are. Sadly, you eat it up. Your ego, speaking in a loud voice, drowns out everything your soft-spoken humility has to say. But your ego isn't speaking the truth. It's telling you only what you want to hear. Your ego totally ignores the lucky breaks that made your 79 possible.

Your ego never mentions the many long putts that you usually miss that you sank. Your ego never mentions the two miraculous chip-ins from the apron. (You'll never again do that twice in a round.) And your ego never mentions the three yanked drives that caromed off trees and came back into play. (That comes to almost ten gifts on your scorecard right there!) And your ego ignores the 98 you fired the very next day. (Perhaps those three pain pills you popped right after that disaster round erased it from your memory.)

Brief flashes of brilliance will swell your ego. A swollen ego — brassy and boisterous — is difficult to manage. When you can't manage your ego, you can't see things clearly. And when you can't see things clearly, you remain ignorant. And when you remain ignorant, you spin your wheels.

Your ignorance represents the dark areas of your psyche — the blind spots. They are your psyche's "I don't know that I don't know zones." Conversely, your awareness, the illuminated areas upstairs, is your "I know that I don't know zone." To stop spinning your wheels, trade your certainty for doubt.

Doubt + Self-awareness = Growth

If you understand neither yourself nor golf, you'll forever spin your wheels. If you understand yourself but not golf or golf but not yourself, you'll spin your wheels periodically. However, if you understand both yourself and golf, you'll rarely spin your wheels. Let me illustrate this abstract point with a brief example. Imagine that you and two friends — Mario and Larry — are playing in a pro-am tournament to support a favorite charity. Your fourth is Jenny, a teaching pro from a local country club.

Mario tees off first. He slices his ball into the right rough. (It's exactly what you expected from Mario.) Mario, a 27-handicapper, plays and practices, but he never seems to improve. When Mario swings a club, he moves everything but his bowels. That's why he shanks the ball. Look closely at his Northwestern irons, and you'll see wear marks on all the hosels. That's why they call Mario "the Hosel Rocket."

If Mario's brain were placed inside the skull of a bird, the bird would fly backward! Mario never bothered to learn the fundamentals. His lack of skill, however, doesn't deter him from giving unsolicited golf advice. The less Mario knows about golf, the more obstinately he knows it. Mario doesn't need lessons — what he needs is a golf lobotomy. Mario is the *unconscious incompetent* member of your group. He understands neither himself nor golf. Poor Mario will forever spin his wheels.

Larry tees off second. His ball caroms off a tree in the left rough and lands on the fairway. If "Lucky Larry" spent his time playing poker in Vegas instead of playing golf, he could afford a house next door to Bill Gates. Larry makes things happen but doesn't know how or why. If you ask Larry how he puts backspin on his wedges, he won't have a clue. Larry is an 18-handicapper who plays remarkably well for someone who never practices.

When Larry booms his drives or hits laser shots with his low irons, you marvel at his gifts. But when he tops his fairway wood and chunks his pitching wedge, you realize how inconsistent he is. One day he can fire an 82, the next day a 102. Larry is the *unconscious competent* member of your foursome. Simply put, Larry doesn't know that he knows. His scores will fluctuate wildly from lucky breaks and sporadic spurts of talent. Consequently, Larry will spin his wheels periodically.

You tee off third. You send your drive about 205 yards over the trap on the right side of the fairway. You're a frustrated 15-handicapper wallowing in uncertainty every time you swing your driver. You lack a complete game, and you know it. Although you putt and chip well, you're not long enough off the tee.

For the past two years, you've been searching to find "the slot" — the position at the top of your swing. That's your Holy Grail. And so you troll golf magazines and monitor the Golf Channel to learn more about the slot. You've identified your weaknesses but can't correct them despite your willingness to do so. You're the *conscious incompetent* member of your group. You don't understand golf, but you do understand yourself. You know that you don't know the swing plane, and that is your advantage over Mario and Larry, even though you, too, will continue to spin your wheels periodically.

Jenny tees off last. She effortlessly cracks her drive 250 yards down the center of the fairway. You're impressed with how confident and relaxed she seems. She possesses the level of golf — an effective and repeatable swing — to which you aspire. Jenny has done her homework. She has worked extremely hard on her game. She learned the correct fundamentals at various PGA schools and became a licensed PGA professional. Jenny is the *conscious competent* member of your group.

Jenny knows that she knows. She gets the job done in all parts of her game and knows why. She knows *what* she needs to learn and *how* to learn it. She understands both herself and golf. She knows enough about golf to hit great shots, and, equally important, she knows enough to self-analyze and self-correct as she goes along. She knows exactly *what* and *how* to practice. She will rarely spin her wheels.

Here's an ancient Arabic proverb on the subject:

He who knows not
    and knows not that he knows not
        is a fool.
            Shun him. [i.e., Mario, the unconscious
                incompetent]

He who knows not
  and knows that he knows not
    is a pupil.
      Teach him. [i.e., you, the conscious
        incompetent]

He who knows
  and knows not that he knows
    is asleep.
      Wake him. [i.e., Larry, the unconscious
        competent]

He [She] who knows
  and knows that he [she] knows
    is a teacher.
      Follow him [her]." [i.e., Jenny,
        the conscious competent]

LAUGH AT YOURSELF

Your ball is teed up much too high. Your driver, sliding under the ball, pops it straight up in the air. It lands at your feet. Or you slice the ball into the rough. A greenskeeper, sitting on his tractor, ducks for cover, then starts waving a white towel. Or your shot goes haywire, ricocheting off the side of the clubhouse. The club pro, hearing the impact, comes out to see who did it. You look around pretending it was somebody else. Or you bend over to mark and clean your ball on the green, and you split your pants. Or you reach to retrieve a nice new ball from a pond, lose your balance, and fall in. Or your shot smacks two trees and lands *behind* you. Tell me — how can you not laugh?

The ability to laugh — especially at yourself — is a great gift. You can't possibly enjoy the richness of golf unless you laugh at yourself. When you laugh about life, it means that you understand life as it is. It means that an inner voice doubts your own importance. It means that you can honestly face what happens to you. It means that you delight in surprises, that you're open and available to the mysteries of golf. "When a thing is funny," George Bernard Shaw wrote, "search it carefully for a hidden truth."

The time your ball caromed off a tree and hit the windshield of the golf cart — where your partner was sipping a beer — offered you an unexpected treat. You couldn't do that again if you tried. When oddities occur, revel in them. Don't try to figure out what happened as if it were a physics problem. Thinking fills you up. Laughing empties you. Become a living mirror — just reflect, don't store. Having a sense of humor on the golf course, Dear Golfer, will help keep you out of the hurt locker.

Laughing (as well as crying) is uniquely human. Animals seemingly don't laugh (or cry); only humans do. Laughter is the most glorious and mysterious human quality. It's life's sweetest music. Aristotle defined man as a rational and thinking animal. But that definition doesn't fly. Your dog is a rational and thinking animal, too. Humans are laughing animals. Laughter is your highest tribute to yourself.

If you become too serious about golf, you demystify it. For the most serious golfers among us, golf is basically a problem-solving exercise. That's when golf becomes hard work. That's when golf becomes a cold piece of business. But golf isn't a problem or a riddle. It's a singular mystery. When you view golf as a mystery, you see its wholeness.

And like golf, laughter is not something you explain. It's something you experience. Laughter — the spontaneous combustion of your spirit — is a mystery as ancient as fire.

The idea of laughing at yourself is a Taoist principle. Taoism's main idea is that everything is *one*. Taoists don't separate things into good and bad, right and wrong, full and empty, hot and cold. By avoiding boundaries and distinctions, Taoists embrace oneness. They believe that opposites converge in all things. Nothing, all by itself, has an independent meaning. Meaning flows from unifying opposites. Coldness means something only in relation to hotness. A low score means something only in relation to a high score.

The fathers of Taoism, Lao-Tzu and Chuang-Tzu, used humor and parable to mock ordinary reasoning and understanding. They believed that deep belly laughter gives a person a glimpse of what life really is — a boundless mystery, an all-encompassing wholeness. This unifying principle of wholeness is called the Tao, meaning "the way." The Tao is not a god or a divine force. It's simply the "way" things are. When Taoists play golf, they don't wrack their brains trying to intellectualize and control everything. Lao-Tzu wrote, "When a foolish man hears of the Tao, he laughs out loud. If he didn't laugh, it wouldn't be the Tao." In a changing and unpredictable universe, learn to laugh.

When a plastic wheel snaps off your pull cart and starts rolling down the cart path, don't ask for an explanation. Just laugh! Luxuriate in the freedom that you don't control everything. Laughter is an expression of that freedom. It's an admission that life is the way it is. Laughing merges you with the big mystery. You're not in control — you never were.

Paradoxically, you can gain control by relinquishing control. As Chuang-Tzu says, you really have no choice. Chuang-Tzu invites golfers to relax, to remain quiet and empty, to find wholeness. When your golf teachers say, "Let the club do the work" or "Take the air out of your hands and arms coming down," they are giving you Taoist advice. They are telling you to gain control by surrendering control.

You may think your short drives are the greatest deficit in your game. Think again. An even greater deficit is your deadly serious mind-set that prevents you from laughing at yourself. Detach yourself periodically to revel in the crazy and hilarious stuff happening around you. If you don't remain open and available to appreciate the totally unexpected elements of golf, you're missing the main attraction. Your score isn't a report card on your life.

When was the last time you laughed uncontrollably? Perhaps it was that windy day when your new Titleist golf hat — purchased in the pro shop an hour before — blew off and got shredded by the mowing tractor coming down the fairway. Everyone laughed hysterically. Do you remember Larry picking up the tattered remains and saying, "I wasn't sure if you wanted to try and sew it back together"?

Laughing lets you glimpse life's hidden wholeness — life's mystery. Laughter reminds you why you are alive in the first place. Would you swap that collective, memorable, and priceless belly laugh for a new $15 golf hat? Let's hope not!

YIN AND YANG

You're looking at a tricky, forty-two-foot putt on the last hole. Your ball rests in the shady hollow of an undulating green whose surface resembles the curved back of a dragon. Your putt has two distinct parts. The first part — moving from shadow to sunlight — is uphill and slow and breaks to the left. The second part is downhill and fast and breaks to the right. To get the ball uphill, you'll have to rap it. However, if you rap it too hard, the ball will roll way past the cup. You're not worried about making this tortuous putt. You're worried about five-putting!

You need an "aggressively cautious" putting stroke (if there is such a thing). This putt must carefully balance up and down, left and right, fast and slow, aggressive and cautious, hard and soft, confident and timid. This putt, like all of golf, is essentially an adventure in balancing opposites.

The Chinese use the terms *yin* and *yang* to express the idea of balancing and unifying opposites. *Yin* and *yang* literally mean the "shady side" and the "sunny side" of a hill, respectively. For Taoists and Confucians, these terms refer to the harmonious interplay of opposite forces or categories. Yin — the female force — is associated with the moon, the poetic, the dark, the moist, the yielding, the weak. Yang — the male force — is associated with the sun, the logical, the light, the dry, the aggressive, the strong. These forces don't oppose or negate each other. Rather, they complement and define each other.

What harmoniously balances and unites these natural forces, according to Taoists, is passive energy (*wu wei*) flowing through invisible earthly (yin) and heavenly (yang) channels called "dragon veins." (Please don't expect clear explanations and definitions from Taoists. The Tao is beyond that!) This passive energy is everywhere even though you can't see, hear, or touch it.

You've probably seen the yin-yang symbol. It consists of a circle divided by an S-curve, which implies flowing and dynamic change. On the white side is a black dot; on the black side, a white dot. This symbol depicts how all things in the universe work. The circle represents the unified and natural cycle of the universe. The black side (yin) and white side (yang) flow into each other as seamlessly and fluidly as night turns into day. The white and black dots suggest that each force contains its opposite.

Each yin-yang symbol is unique. Some have two unequal or lopsided halves. They were deliberately made that way. The uneven division denotes the ebb and flow of nature. For example, winter days have more darkness (yin), and summer days have more sunlight (yang). Spring days have more moisture (yin), and autumn days have more dryness (yang). The yin-yang circle depicts nature's dynamic state.

Taking a yin-yang perspective will allow you to see golf with new eyes. Marcel Proust wrote, "The real voyage of discovery consists not in seeking new landscapes, but in having new eyes." Learn to start looking at familiar things with fresh eyes. When you view golf or anything else with fresh eyes, you often find some unexpected truths.

A yin-yang perspective may help you understand your emotional state. Golf as a yin-yang experience is both static and dynamic, beautiful and dreadful, messy and tidy, chaotic and orderly, comforting and heartbreaking, serene and troubling, logical and crazy all at the same time! If golf were otherwise, you probably wouldn't play.

How many times have your emotions flip-flopped when your putt — rolling dead-straight for the hole — inexplicably lips out? (When this happens to Peter — my emotional, Greek golfing friend — he turns to me in disbelief and says, "Hey! What the hell is this *garbage?*") Conversely, how many times have you cursed yourself for flubbing a putt that miraculously plops in? Your golf emotions, as the yin-yang circle implies, are in constant flux. Some days your circle contains more yin, or darkness — on other days, more yang, or light.

The richness of golf lies in the interplay of opposites — in sunlight and shadow, in land and water, in hills and valleys, in stillness and chatter, in still air and wind, in short grass and rough, in sunshine and rain, in dawn and dusk. Without opposites golf would be dreadfully dull.

Most important, taking a yin-yang perspective will help your golf swing. Taking a yin-yang swing-perspective prompted a quantum leap in my game. Learning to balance left and right, upper and lower, backswing and downswing, passive and active forces, I gained greater power and distance. Viewing my swing from a yin-yang perspective, I discovered how a golfer can swing effortlessly *and* hit the ball far. Once you learn this secret, you'll feel like Harry Potter at the Hogwarts School for Witchcraft and Wizardry when he first learns to cast magical spells.

Having studied and played golf for decades, I contend that a yin-yang perspective — focused on balancing and unifying opposites — is the best way to build a low-maintenance swing. To build a repeatable and effective swing, you need to balance and unify opposing and complementary forces: left/right, upper/lower, passive/active, tension/relaxation, body/mind, linear/rotational, and so on.

The Buddha claimed that his job was only "to point the way." He advised his followers to work out their own salvation with their own diligence. I wish to do the same. Once I "point the way," you'll need to work out your own golf salvation by diligently reviewing the other key parts of your swing, such as the grip, stance, posture, weight shift, swing plane, and wrist action.

A major power principle of the golf swing is that of *torsion* — twisting one part of your body and resisting with another part along a fixed axis. By doing that, you generate power.

Torsion is easy to illustrate. Imagine you're swinging an ax or a baseball bat. Would you swing the ax or bat by coiling your entire body at one time and at one speed? I doubt it! To generate power, you need torsion. So too with the golf club. You need to twist some body parts and resist with others. Simply put, the secret to gaining a powerful swing is through torsion — balancing sequentially the yin (resistance) and yang (twisting) forces of your body.

Ben Hogan knew this, although he never referred to yin and yang. But he did warn golfers about overrotating their hips — perhaps the most common flaw among all golfers. And that is a yin-yang principle. When you overrotate your hips, you eliminate the resistance factor. Hogan demonstrated the concept of torsion in a famous illustration. A right-handed golfer has a large rubber band attached to his left hip. The other end of the rubber band is attached to a wall. The rubber band — illustrating left-hip resistance at takeaway — was Hogan's way to convey the yin-yang principle of balancing the forces associated with twisting and resisting.

Admittedly, Bobby Jones, Sam Snead, and other great golfers have overrotated (swiveled) their hips. However, they were the exceptions. Hogan was definitely correct: overrotating will drain your power. In your one-plane swing, learn to *balance* resistance and twisting. Make your swing operate like a catapult, a slingshot, or a crossbow. If you eliminate the resistance factor, your swing will operate like a rubber crutch.

You create torsion by opposing specific muscles at specific stages of the swing. Trying to understand how your muscles work in the golf swing is not easy. For example, if you want to understand how to swing like Ernie Els, ideally you need to be inside Ernie's body. It's not enough to see how Ernie's muscles work. You need to feel his muscles swinging. Quite simply, you can't readily see the resistance Ernie creates in his muscles. Even if he removed his shirt, you might not see his back muscles twisting and coiling. Also, you can't see the resistance he creates on the insteps of his feet, in his thighs, and in his knees.

If you could enter the body of most tour pros, you would feel them creating torsion by opposing specific muscles at specific stages of the swing. You would feel the power of pulling away with one side and resisting with the other. The yin-yang of the swing is simply one of resistance and pull. Unless you create resistance, you'll have nothing to hit against.

Read Jimmy Ballard's book *How to Perfect Your Golf Swing: Using Connection and the Seven Common Denominators*. Although the book never refers to yin and yang, I immediately viewed Ballard's coil-and-recoil description of the golf swing from a Taoist perspective. The most useful thing I learned from Ballard involved the yin-yang activity of the hips. Specifically, I learned to keep my hips balanced and level — not too much or too little lateral movement.

Ballard talks about coiling from inside your right hip against a braced right knee. He refers to this as "loading the gun." Ballard teaches his pupils to use opposing and complementary yin-yang forces — resistance/bracing versus torsion/coiling — to create power.

Yin-yang forces, according to the Taoists, remain in the body until death. At death, the yang goes back to heaven and the yin goes back to earth. At that point, yin and yang are ready for recycling. Perhaps the same thing happens to expired golfers. One part goes back to earth and the other part goes to heaven. As you stand over the ball — your feet on the ground and your head skyward — ponder the yin-yang forces moving in your dragon veins.

THE FOUR KINDS OF HORSES

A famous Eastern parable describes four different kinds of horses: excellent, good, poor, and bad. The excellent horse responds as soon as it sees the moving shadow of the driver's whip. The good horse responds when it senses the first touch of the whip. The poor horse responds when it feels the sting of the whip. And the bad horse responds only when it feels the lash of the whip deep in the marrow of its bones.

When you hear this parable, you immediately want to identify with the excellent horse, right? But that's not what this parable is about. The issue is not whether you want to be the excellent, good, poor, or bad horse. When you practice and play golf, how you wish to identify yourself, good or bad, is not what matters. What's important is that you identify who you really are and act from that place. There are different kinds of golfers, and you must know which one you are.

Your biggest job, in golf and in life, is to find out who you really are. One of the greatest harms you can inflict on yourself is to trick yourself into believing you are someone you aren't. When you muster the courage to look at yourself clearly and honestly, you make it possible to grow. Your golf game will allow you to learn what kind of "horse" you really are.

Whatever your level of golf, that is your real golf-self at that moment. That is also your strength, even if you're not very good. If you delude yourself into thinking that you're an excellent or good golfer, then you will stagnate. The parable is not about striving harder to become the best golfer you can be. The message here is about seeing yourself clearly and honestly. Seeing yourself honestly will inspire you to work harder.

Your real golf identity is who you are right now. Admit it and go on from there. To know and to honor your true golf identity is essentially to make peace with yourself. Knowing your true golf identity is the first step in fulfilling your potential. You will grow when you become an honest observer of yourself. Unfortunately, finding out what kind of horse you really are is something you have to do on your own.

"LEARNING IS THE THING FOR YOU"

Chuck, one of my golfing companions, told me something astonishing. Chuck has played in a Thursday golf league with the same eighty members for decades. Since 1976 he has thanklessly recorded and posted their handicaps. When Chuck recently went back over his records, he made a startling discovery. He learned that every member has maintained essentially the same handicap for thirty years! Except for members experiencing injury or illness, every single one still has the same handicap that he started with!

How can this be? For thirty years these golfers have played, practiced, read instructional books, subscribed to golf magazines, updated their equipment, taken private lessons, studied instructional videos, video-analyzed their swings, attended golf schools, watched the Golf Channel, and received expert tips. But not a single one has improved his level of proficiency. Think about that.

How is it possible to perform the same task — square dancing, woodworking, weight lifting, cycling, karate, quilting — for decades and never improve? Imagine being a member of a karate studio for thirty years. During your second month, you earn your yellow belt. And for the next thirty years, you never earn another belt. After all that time, you leave the karate studio with basically the same skills that you started with, and all you have to show for it is a yellow belt!

The simple truth is that golfers can be divided into learners and nonlearners. Whether you're a learner or nonlearner is entirely up to you.

Casey Eberting — an enlightened teacher who operates a golf school in Texas hill country — says that only one golfer in a thousand (if that) improves significantly once he or she reaches a certain point. And what is that certain point? When do your golf skills reach a plateau? When do you stop improving? According to one study, golfers stop improving after three years.

Think about the implications here. Let's assume that your golf career lasts for forty years. So you'll spend your first three years improving and the remaining thirty-seven stagnating. That means that 92 percent of your golf career will be spent stagnating. Unless you have some physical impairment, why don't you improve?

If you don't marshal your learning powers, you won't improve. To improve you need to wake up and start paying close attention to what works, what doesn't, and why. Start moving in the direction of continuous learning. All it requires is following this simple formula:

$$\text{Learning} = \text{Discovery} + \text{Mastery}$$

Discovery is the process of forming an accurate picture of the world. To improve your swing, you need an accurate picture of both your swing and the "ideal" swing. Only when you have this accurate picture can you make intelligent comparisons and corrections. Astute comparisons are the stuff of growth.

Discovery means reconciling your swing with the ideal swing. The ideal swing incorporates sound fundamentals, conforms to theoretical principles, and produces effective and repeatable results. The ideal swing is like a door — it opens and closes smoothly, functions simply, and requires little or no maintenance.

The only way to understand the golf swing's many nuances, complexities, mysteries, minute details, and hidden secrets is to look deeply and ask questions. There's no other way. Learning to swing a golf club is a challenging task. Discovery takes considerable time, effort, and patience, so don't expect immediate results.

Discovery is both self-guided and expert-guided. To gain an accurate picture of yourself and the ideal, rely both on yourself and on experts. Start the discovery process by looking deeply and asking questions about your swing. When you openly and honestly take a look at exactly what's happening in your swing, you will start to grow. Simultaneously, ask questions about the ideal swing by consulting a variety of resources. Use your awareness and curiosity to discover your ideal swing.

Of the many issues to consider on your guided path of discovery, learn the difference between *swinging* and *hitting*. In his 1937 book *Swinging into Golf*, Ernest Jones wrote, "The golf swing is a measure of time that few people ever learn to pace." Unless you know how your body should behave (what certain body parts should do and when), you won't be able to learn the pace or timing of your swing. A swing honors time — a hit destroys time. Discover what timing is all about.

What resources (instructors, books, videos, schools, etc.) should guide your discovery process? Frankly, there are no right sources. There are sources that speak to your nature and those that don't. Consider a number of expert resources to help you form an accurate picture of swing theory and swing fundamentals. Goethe said, "We cannot possess something we do not understand." Accordingly, form an accurate picture of the mechanical laws associated with the golf swing.

What happens during that 1/1,000th of a second when clubhead and ball collide? In *The Physics of the Golf Swing*, Theodore Jorgensen, a retired physics professor, claims that the laws of physics and the limitations of your body determine a correct golf swing. What's really important about Jorgensen is not his book and its complicated terms and equations but his approach. Learn from Jorgensen that your golf swing boils down to basic laws of physics.

Consult user-friendly resources that will explain the laws of "conservation of angular momentum" and "centrifugal force." From your guided tour of basic physics, you'll learn that the longer the ball stays on the clubface, the better you'll hit it. Explore swing fundamentals (grip, stance, posture, alignment, swing plane) by consulting a variety of resources. All golf schools, expert instructors, authoritative texts, and videos are not equal. Be prepared to read between the lines and fill in the blanks. Often your resources will intentionally or unintentionally omit and obscure valuable pieces of information. Expose yourself to a range of resources. Be selective, critical, and open to possibilities.

Attribute *intentional* omissions and obscurities in your resources to their reluctance to share publicly what took them considerable time and sweat to discover. If you found a cave filled with buried treasure, would you publish and sell a $6.99 paperback revealing the contents and location of that treasure? It's the same with golfers who find buried treasures, including Ben Hogan.

Look for contradictions *within* resources. Let's say your

resource (a private instructor or author) advises you to assume a particular upright posture. Yet your resource doesn't exhibit (in person or in photos) that same upright posture. In such cases, pay closer attention to what the resource does and less attention to what the resource says.

Look for consistencies and inconsistencies *among* resources. When you discover that your resources are essentially saying the same things — in different ways — you're on to something.

Expect to find undefined and vague terms along the way. Suppose your resource advises you to turn your hips or shoulders "horizontally." Does your resource mean horizontal to the ground? Horizontal to your spine angle? To resolve these ambiguities, study the accompanying photos and ask probing questions. Compare resources. They will provide mostly clues, not complete answers.

In the discovery process, expect the unexpected. Hogan wrote, "Reverse every natural instinct you have and just do the opposite of what you are inclined to do and you will probably come very close to having a perfect golf swing." Hogan advises you to shift your focus. If you're not improving, you may be looking in the wrong direction. Try focusing on the unfamiliar, the unnatural, the uncomfortable.

Discover *actively* by asking questions, taking notes, "talking back," looking deeply, and digesting things slowly and systematically. Active discoverers constantly ask *why* and *what if*. All productive learning involves conducting an ongoing internal dialogue with yourself. Ask *why*, for example, this resource is advising you to hinge or cock your wrists early in the backswing. *What if* you hinged or cocked your wrists at the top?

In T.H. White's book *The Once and Future King*, young Arthur, who is experiencing his dark night of the soul, seeks advice from Merlin, his mentor. Merlin's apt answer applies to golfers. He tells Arthur:

> The best thing for being sad is to learn something. That's the only thing that never fails. You may grow old and trembling in your anatomies. You may lie awake at night listening to the disorder in your veins. You may miss your only love. You may see the world around you devastated by evil lunatics. . . . There's only one thing for it, then: To Learn! Learn why the world wags and what wags it. That is the only thing which the mind can never exhaust, never alienate, never be tortured by, never fear or distrust, and never dream of forgetting. Learning is the thing for you.

Learn how the golf swing wags and what wags it. Learn your swing and the ideal swing. Then draw intelligent comparisons and make practical adjustments.

Also, discover the vocabulary of the golf swing. Learn the key terms — the transactional vocabulary of the swing (torque, ground forces, centrifugal force, the lever system, resistance, swing plane, strong grip, shoulder turn, hinging the wrists, cupping the wrists, setting the wrists).

To drive your car, you don't need to know the names of all its parts and how they work. However, to repair your car, you must know the parts and how they work. If you only want to swing the club, don't bother learning key terms and swing theory. However, if you want to repair your golf swing, learn the key terms of swing theory and fundamentals.

Consult reputable and savvy local instructors and texts by distinguished teachers such as David Leadbetter, Nick Bradley, Jim Flick, Jim McLean, Jim Hardy, Joe Dante, and John Jacobs.

Many books have guided my discovery process, especially Dante's *Four Magic Moves to Winning Golf* and Hardy's *Plane Truth for Golfers*. Although Dante's diagrams and photos need work, his book helped me see the big picture, understand golf's main fallacies, and comprehend swing theory.

Hardy's book helped me grasp the two sets of fundamentals associated with the swing plane. One-planers swing their shoulders and clubhead on the same plane. Two-planers swing on two planes simultaneously — their shoulders move horizontally while their arms move vertically.

According to Hardy, you mix oil and water if you match up the wrong set of fundamentals. If you're not improving, you may be mixing oil and water. When you learn the correct set of fundamentals associated with your one-plane or two-plane swing, you'll start to improve.

Certain resources — golf schools, lessons, books, and videos — represent systematic approaches. Magazines, on the other hand, provide you with a piecemeal approach. Even though they can play an important role in your guided discovery process, they give you only pieces. You must decide whether these pieces actually fit your system. Read and respond to articles selectively, especially if the resource is a one-planer and you're a two-planer or if the resource's unique personal parameters (age, flexibility, build) don't match yours.

Carry a small notebook in your golf bag to record your discoveries. After a good round or practice session, take notes on what you discovered. If you find a buried treasure, how can you locate it again if you don't draw yourself a map?

Mastery follows discovery in the learning process. Mastery means making your discoveries second nature, routine, automatic, effortless, and efficient. Without mastery, discovery is pointless. What good is it to discover proper swing techniques yet never learn how to implement them? What good is it to find a buried treasure yet never possess it?

Norman Bryant, a Mississippi teaching pro, tells his pupils, "I can show you the swing in ten minutes — and you can spend the rest of your life learning it."

Your degree of mastery depends on your response to two questions:

1. What do you wish to achieve?
2. What are you willing to do to achieve it?

Responding to the first question is a snap. You want long drives, straight shots, solid ball striking, low scores, and trophies. Responding to the second question, however, ultimately determines your destiny. Precious few golfers are prepared to invest the time and energy to attain mastery. Golfers want immediate results. Unfortunately, learning how to play golf and getting immediate results don't coincide.

The "Hogan ethos" is all about hard work. Hogan refused to give private lessons. He said that "he couldn't find anyone who wanted to learn." Don't misunderstand Hogan's point. He didn't mean that people are uninterested in learning. He meant that people aren't prepared to make the effort to gain mastery. Hogan claimed, "The answers are in the dirt." He meant that learning golf — both discovering and mastering the game — takes inordinate time and energy spent hitting practice balls.

Mastery of the swing often begins with slow-motion swings — again and again and again. Mastery then takes the form of swinging normally — again and again and again. Mastery eventually means hitting practice balls — again and again and again. Expect to hit lots of bad shots. Expect things to get worse before they get better. Expect to get frustrated. Expect to feel uncomfortable as you ask your body to adopt new ways of doing things. Swing changes are like root canals and divorces. Be prepared for some short-term pain in exchange for some long-term relief.

When you practice, don't mix swing fundamentals from different resources. Don't mix Hardy's set of swing fundamentals with Leadbetter's set during your practices. Stick with one, understand it, then move to another. Practice one set of fundamentals long enough to understand, practice, and implement them.

However, mastery means not only technique but also attitude. Ask yourself probing questions. For example, do you simply want a bandage for your slice? Or do you actually want to cure your slice? Do you want to compensate for your lousy grip? Or do you actually want to fix your lousy grip? Your degree of mastery depends entirely on what you're willing to risk and invest.

Total mastery requires a total commitment. There's nothing wrong with partial commitments. We all can't become Ben Hogan. However, there are different forms and degrees of commitment. Commitments are like wagers. Pathetically small wagers yield pathetically small rewards. What you're prepared to wager is your business. But know this — if you never wager anything worth a damn, you'll never win big.

Claude Harmon tells the students attending his golf school, "You can't be a thoroughbred, but I can make you a racing mule." When his students graduate, Harmon gives them a certificate of induction into "The Society of Racing Mules."

Rare golfers become thoroughbreds. Select golfers become racing mules. The overwhelming majority of golfers, however, remain mules. Mules are stubborn draft animals that learn how to pull a barge or plow a field.

ANGER

The moment you let anger take over your golf game, you are no longer in charge. Anger is. And anger will inevitably dictate what happens next — whether you like it or not. The key to dealing with anger is not just to shut it down or ignore it but to see it clearly for what it is and to harness it constructively. Anger may become your biggest weakness or your biggest strength, depending on how you deal with it. If you look deeply inside your anger, you'll find wisdom.

Your anger contains a wealth of emotion and energy. The very emotion and energy that allow you to play well are the same emotion and energy that can destroy you. The emotion that makes you angry is the same one that makes you passionate, exciting, and interesting. So don't get rid of it — make friends with it.

Let's say you hook your tee shot out-of-bounds on the first hole. Or you miss a simple gimme-putt to lose the match. Or you airmail the green with a wedge from sixty yards, and the ball lands in a brook. Naturally, you become angry. But let's look inside your anger. It has two parts: the thoughts and the emotional energy beneath the thoughts. When you blow your top, you replay your thoughts again and again. It's like replaying a tragic movie, and you're the star. Your thoughts conduct an ongoing conversation inside you. By continuing them, you block the awareness to deal with the emotional energy beneath the thought.

Think of anger this way: let's say you just replaced a leaky cold-water valve in your basement. Unknowingly, you over-tightened and cracked the new valve. When you open the main to test the valve, water gushes all over. Naturally, you get angry. You start yelling at the wrench and the lousy valve that the idiot at the hardware store sold you. Your thoughts go berserk. "Why did I have to tighten the valve so much?" "Why didn't my father-in-law return my smaller pipe wrench so this didn't happen in the first place?" "Why can't people return stuff that they borrow — the way I always do?" "Why do hardware stores sell lousy valves like this anyway?" "They can put a man on the moon, but can't make a decent valve?" "Why do disasters like this always have to happen to me?"

As you rant and rave, water continues to gush everywhere, and your basement floods. The best thing for you to do is to shut off the main. Have the awareness to go to the source of the problem. The longer you continue your internal conversation, the longer you will remain angry and miserable. In this case, the source is the water main. In golf, the source is yourself. Awareness is the act of going back to yourself. The only medicine for anger is awareness. You can remain angry on the golf course only if you are unaware of your source. It's impossible to be angry and aware at the same time. You can't manage anger and awareness together. Awareness cuts to the root of anger.

After a poor shot or a disastrous hole, stop interacting with others and yourself. Move beyond the rambling internal conversation. Address the source. The more your thoughts rage, the more your emotions flare. Your muscles tighten when you are angry. If anger remains inside you, it acts like liquid drain cleaner in your veins. It will scorch your insides. Unvented and unaddressed, anger will create the ultimate poison facing all golfers — tension.

Let's say you hit a ball in the water or deep into the woods. Then you start to beat yourself up over it! You can't let go of your anger. You feel like a helpless victim of rage. But that's not the case at all. You're using a bad shot to rationalize your anger. Getting bent out of shape over a bad shot is like getting angry over a nasty memo that you wrote to yourself. You create your own thoughts. Thinking isn't something that happens to you. Thinking is something you do yourself. You create your anger by listening and clinging to your own thinking. You can make yourself a victim on the golf course without much effort.

Awareness is the key to cooling your anger. Awareness means opening your mind and heart. Experience your anger fully, then let it go. To be angry is to be human. Even the Dalai Lama and the Pope get angry. So lighten up. Breathe in and out a few times and smile at yourself the way Fuzzy Zoeller does when he plays. Smiling will give you tremendous relief. I am a reluctant flyer. Smiling is the only way I can relieve the tension that flying creates in me. I don't use tranquilizers or hypnosis to relax. I just breathe rhythmically and smile.

Where does anger come from? According to some Eastern thinkers, anger arises from three illusions. First, it's the illusion that things are changeless. (Don't expect things to remain the same. Your pipes and your golf game are always changing.) Second, it's the illusion that the world and you are separate. (Don't expect the world to change while you stay the same. Your pipes and your game change like everyone else's.) Third, it's the illusion that happiness is long-lived. (Don't expect to remain happy indefinitely. Your pipes and your game will invariably leak. Things fall apart.)

Anger is a parasite. It can't exist all by itself. Emotions —

anger, lust, greed, fear — need your life-energy to exist and grow. For anger to grow, you have to identify with it. You've nourished it with your energy and attention. However, if you refuse to feed it, your anger will pass harmlessly like a cloud in the sky or a leaf in the brook.

When Eastern thinkers use the term *nonidentification*, they mean refusing to feed your emotions. It means breaking your connection with certain thoughts or emotions. When you get angry on the course, take a step back and remain aloof. Just imagine your anger being played out on a movie screen in your head. Let it roll by. Become an impartial watcher, not a host for your anger. Otherwise, it will be like a tapeworm.

If you put a mirror too close to your eyes, you can't see your face. So too with anger. To observe it, you need a certain distance. When you and your anger are too close, they become one. Simply put, your emotions are like parasites feeding off the life-energy that "identification" creates for them.

Get to know your anger completely and gently. Get comfortable with being uncomfortable. You can't run away from the anger inside you. You have to accept it. Become a bubble riding a rolling, powerful, crashing ocean wave. Ride out the wave. Then let go of your anger. Walk the course calmly and mindfully. Become aware of slowing down your breathing. Become attentive to each peaceful inhale and exhale.

Once your breathing steadies you, label your emotion precisely for what it is: "anger." It is nothing more or less. Don't make judgments about it. It's neither good nor bad. It's just anger. It's a part of you that makes you human, precious, and unique. Open your mind and heart and become friends with your anger. "Hello, Anger — I know you are in there. How are you, Anger, my golf partner, my old friend?" Let the anger run its course and drift away like the mist in the morning.

NAVAJO SUN, GOLF SUN

The Navajo teach their children that a new sun is born each day. It lives for only twenty-four hours. At sunset, when it dies, it will never return again. When Navajo children are old enough to understand this notion, their parents sit with them at dawn and wait for the sun to rise.

At first light, the parents tell their children that the sun has only *today* to live. To not waste the sun's precious and sacred rays, the children are told to live this day in a special way. On only this particular day will this particular sun shine down on them. To waste a single precious moment of their day is to dishonor the sun by letting it die before it was ever fully used.

If you view the sun as Navajos do, you won't waste a single moment when you play golf. Your golf game will become a succession of precious moments. If you become miserable and depressed, you'll waste the sun shining down on you. Your resentment and disappointment with your score will prevent you from appreciating the hot smell of pines at noon or the fresh green of spring. Remind yourself that you're never going to have this golf moment again. Give thanks. Nothing is worth more than this moment. Rumi, the thirteenth-century poet, wrote, "There are one hundred ways to kneel and kiss the earth."

Remind yourself that you're never going to have this golf moment again. How can you possibly be upset knowing that these beautiful things all around you are so steady, so simple? The fairways ever growing. The wind ever stirring the branches. The trees ever shading the course. The wildflowers ever sprouting in the rough. The birds ever singing. The water ever sparkling in the sun.

Magnify the obvious. "If the stars should appear one night in a thousand years," Ralph Waldo Emerson wrote, "how men would believe and adore!" Your thoughts shape your personality. What you cherish ultimately defines who you are.

You are totally present with golf when you ask yourself, "Have I ever been this happy before?" When you feel enraptured — fully absorbed in time and place without a hint of ego or judgment — you are in what the ancient Greeks called "kairos." That's when time stops. Rumi called that same rapture "the secret sky within our hearts."

"The Seventh Direction" is a legend passed on by Native American storytellers. They describe how the Great Spirit quickly established the six directions of north, south, east, west, above, and below. Then the Great Spirit had to decide where to establish the most important direction, the Seventh Direction, containing power and wisdom. The Great Spirit selected a secret place where humans would never think to look — inside their own hearts! This story illustrates the point that wisdom is not something that you need to create from scratch: it's something already inside you that you need to discover.

Remember to open your heart. Use each golf day to connect your life passion with your golf passion. The sun — born to shine on only this particular day — will die this evening. Every day is special just as it is. Don't waste it.

DRINK THE ICE WATER

During a round of golf under a midday August sun, my foursome finally arrived at the oasis. But George, my partner, hot and thirsty, refused a welcome drink from the water jug. He had scored a double-bogey on the previous hole, a fairly easy par-5. He decided to punish himself by going without a drink of water. He was so concerned about his score, he was unable to enjoy either the golf or even a cold drink. He simply couldn't forgive himself. "George," I said, "put your ass in neutral, calm down, and drink some ice water." He refused.

The point of playing golf rests not on the tip of a pencil recording your score. Golf isn't successful if it gives you low scores. Golf is successful if it's growth enhancing.

Let's face it — golf is rarely the way you want it to be. Golf is simply the way it is. Golf may be the ultimate reconciliation with the self. And if you free the self from inevitable mistakes, you will begin to appreciate your humanness. Golf is the great equalizer. Not because it makes us all play equally, but because it exposes equally the weaknesses and insecurities of us all. Even those of Tiger Woods, Ernie Els, Freddie Couples, and Vijay Singh.

The only way to grow is to forgive your golf mistakes. Your forgiveness returns you to yourself. Steady growth happens only through conscious nurturing. Golf growth — or any growth — doesn't happen all by itself. You make it happen. "The way I change my life," Ashley Montague wrote, "is to act as if I'm the person I want to be."

If you crave only lower scores, longer drives, and straighter irons, you will anguish over golf. Anguish arises when you desire something other than what you already have. Cut yourself some slack and admit it: you rarely get the golf you want.

Golf is an adventure in forgiveness. Before your round, absolve all your golf mistakes *in advance*. Forgive yourself before you start. People spend years in therapy trying to forgive themselves. By forgiving your errant shots in advance, you loosen the bonds of expectation and make friends with yourself.

What ultimately gets entered in "The Great Book of Golf" is not your score but how successful you were in expressing your growth, your wholeness, your joy, and your love for the game. Make every day your best golf day. This is your life right now.

You're human, my friend. Drink the ice water — it's hot out there!

"BE THOU A HAPPY GOLFER?"

Diogenes, an ancient Greek philosopher who belonged to a school known as the Cynics, walked around Athens every afternoon in search of an honest man. According to legend, Diogenes carried a lantern and looked deeply into the faces of his fellow Athenians. To every man he approached, Diogenes asked the same burning question: "Be thou an honest man?"

Apparently, Diogenes never found an honest man. His fruitless quest, leaving him bitter and skeptical about his generation, had a profound effect on him. Diogenes, accompanied by only his dogs, wound up taking residence in a large wooden tub, wearing coarse robes, sleeping on the bare ground, eating only plain foods, and sneering at his fellow citizens. He turned into a sour old man.

If you asked this Cynic today to find not an honest man but a happy golfer, his search would be even harder. Picture Diogenes carrying his lantern and traversing the golf courses of the world on sunny afternoons, looking for a happy golfer. What would you say if Diogenes approached you on the golf course, held up his lantern to your face, and asked, "Be thou a happy golfer?"

I don't know what you would say. But most serious golfers of my acquaintance might tell Diogenes something like this: "No, I'm not *happy*! Can't you see I'm trying to putt. Now get your lantern, your mangy dog, and your sorry butt off this green. And stop asking ridiculous questions!"

Sages — ancient and modern alike — have claimed that happiness flows from fulfilling your expectations. Conversely, when your expectations remain unfulfilled, unhappiness follows. Golf is all about expectations. What does your list of expectations include? How about longer drives, lower scores, smoother swings, fewer putts, tighter chip shots, fuller shoulder turns, longer backswings, looser grip pressure, better footwork, higher pitches, slower takeaway, more sand saves, more victories, more greens in regulation, more fairways hit, and, God willing, at least one hole in one before the inevitable onset of senility, infirmity, or death!

There's no problem in trying to fulfill your goals and desires. The problem occurs when you fail to take delight in the agonizing struggle and drudgery along the way. When you become so fixated on your expectations, you leave little room inside for joy.

What if, however, you never satisfy your expectations? According to statistics published recently by the National Golf Foundation, the score of the average golfer for an 18-hole round is about 100. Surprisingly, this score hasn't changed in over twenty years. Despite the technological advances in equipment and the increase in accessibility of golf instruction and analysis — the Golf Channel, tapes, videos, magazines, books, computer graphics, and so forth — the score of the average golfer has not improved in over two decades.

But let's look on the positive side. Let's say you do improve dramatically. You succeed in attaining your immediate goals and desires. Does that mean that you achieve golf nirvana? Probably not. Most likely, you'll just establish new expectations and restart the whole miserable process. Your frustration will continue. Lowering your handicap or scoring average is like winning the Mega-Bucks or Super Lotto. The instant you win the jackpot, you're elated. But the elation is short-lived. You'll quickly realize that the jackpot isn't enough. Despite winning all that money, you'll discover that you're still miserable.

Naturally, you expect this jackpot will make you happy. But it won't. It never does. Why? Because the jackpot isn't happiness. The jackpot — like fame, romance, power — is something you *associate* with happiness. The jackpot is external. Happiness is internal.

For many years, I was fixated on achieving certain goals. Consequently, I programmed myself for unhappiness. My golf motto was the same one used at Harvard's Business School: "What matters, gets measured. And what gets measured, gets managed." For decades I adopted a "measure-and-manage" model of golf. According to my narrow model, I saw only what I expected to see, only what made sense, only what looked familiar, only what was measurable.

No more! My new golf motto, which was also reportedly tacked on Einstein's office bulletin board, reads as follows: "Not everything that counts can be counted. And not everything that can be counted counts."

Previously, all I cared about was the scorecard. However, my scorecard became my WMD — my "weapon of *math* destruction." My measure-and-manage approach resulted in what psychologists call inattention blindness. I didn't see what was right under my nose. My golf world was congruent only with the model I created. My brain didn't process and organize all data equally. It processed and organized *only* the golf data that fit my model. And so my model — riveted on the measurable and the analytic — never processed the unmeasurable and the sublime.

I eventually decided to change my mental model. You may want to do the same. In my new model, I don't leave my happiness to chance. I actively cultivate and nurture it, like seeds in my garden. I don't let the quality of my performance solely determine my level of happiness. Essentially, I take control of my happiness.

Of course, there are many things in golf that you can't control — the gusting wind, the large fairway bunker, the long par-5s, the narrow fairway, the fast green, or the heavy dew on the grass. However, your happiness is one key thing you *can* help control. As soon as you deprogram yourself, you're no longer a helpless victim on a treadmill of unhappiness. To get off the treadmill, you need to provide a whole new set of rewards for yourself.

Your happiness in golf depends ultimately on your inner harmony and ability to find joy in the events of each moment. Happiness often happens because you program it to happen. If you're only happy when a rare eagle, birdie, or par putt drops in the cup, you are storing your joy in a coffin.

When Nancy Lopez first joined the LPGA Tour, her father gave her some great advice: "Play happy!" What better advice can any golfer receive? You must let your passion spill over — otherwise it's incomplete. Your happiness flows from understanding what compels you to play golf in the first place. Let your happiness spread its roots deeply into your heart. Create a miniature Magic Kingdom inside yourself.

Decide for yourself what golf means. Don't borrow someone else's meaning. Golf means what you want it to mean. Golf is a blank scorecard, an empty page, an open canvas. The meaning of golf is the meaning you bring to it, that you create for it. Golf means whatever you say it means. So why not define golf as blissfully as you can?

Most important, consider defining golf in terms of *balance*. Ultimately, golf is all about balance. Balancing your weight at address. Your grip pressure. Your left and right sides. The speed of your swing. Movement and stillness. Relaxation and power. Composure and tension. Anger and serenity. Head and heart. Performance and enjoyment. Birdies and double bogeys. If you're happy, you're essentially in balance.

How can golfers, amid such beautiful landscapes, be so chronically unhappy and out of whack? How can a golf course, whose natural forces are so life-giving, be so death-dealing? If you get continually upset out there, then wake up! Being miserable is the surest sign you're out of balance — that you're missing what life is all about. Open your awareness and access the vanishing, precious, and sublime things all around you.

Open your eyes to golf's transcendent moments: the walk to the clubhouse at dusk with a close friend. The shadows of twilight on the green. The red-tailed hawk circling high above. The mown grass and early dew underfoot. The smell of pine straw. The morning mist hanging over the fairway. Golf's unmeasurables, the richest of its treasures, reveal themselves when you're open and available to receive them. That's when you're living large — when golf becomes sacred, when everything merits your attention and respect.

Being happy means staying in balance. Golf was not invented to fulfill your desires and goals. Golf is just another way to challenge your mettle, test your character, humble your ego, and confront your limitations. It isn't an end in itself. It's a preparation and a testing ground for something much larger. If you're too serious, too grasping, too needy, you'll make yourself miserable. So chill out.

Imagine Diogenes approaching you on the course. When he lifts up his lantern, looks you straight in the eye, and asks if you're a happy golfer, what will you say? If you can answer affirmatively, you've passed golf's final exam. The brief answer to golf's final-exam question — "Are you a happy golfer?" — goes something like this: "Absolutely, yes! Despite my hapless failures, my countless limitations, my innumerable frustrations, and my slavish addiction to golf's endless drudgery, I nonetheless derive immense moment-by-moment joy along the way."

When Diogenes hears your words and sees a smile bud on your lips, he'll pack up and head home. His search will be over. He will have found what he was searching for. He'll have found you, a happy golfer!

THE INTERNAL METRONOME

Inside you is a path of energy that flows down the front of your body and up your spine. (Eastern thinkers like to refer to the life force as energy.) This energy, pulsating and vibrating within you, forms the essence of your mind, senses, emotions, and physical body. It is at the core of all your thoughts, feelings, and actions.

When people practice yoga, they make a conscious effort to feel and to channel this flow of energy. Golfers need to do the same thing. Becoming aware of your energies, you will learn to relax and to mobilize your resources. You can view yourself and your world, in short, as waves of energy.

When you are angry or tense on the course, your energy becomes blocked. You may literally feel tightness in your throat or chest. When you learn to become aware of your energy flow, however, you shift your attention away from the physical world and toward the inner self.

By taking your attention inside, you become attuned to the energy that supports the physical world. An awareness of your energy flow will direct your consciousness away from the external factors of ball or club or score and toward the inner resource of self.

You do not have to create this circuit of energy. It already exists. Waves of energy periodically flow through your spine. As long as you live, these pulsations are like the beats of a metronome. A metronome, a device with an inverted pendulum, beats time to maintain tempo when you practice playing a musical instrument. A sliding weight on the pendulum regulates the tempo.

Your own breathing is like a metronome. Your willful act to regulate your breathing is like a sliding weight. Whether you are learning piano or golf, tempo is very important. Many golfers, including myself, use a metronome to develop a smooth and rhythmic putting stroke. Unfortunately, you can't put a metronome beside you on the green when you putt. You have to have a metronome inside you.

The energy pulsating up your spine forms the pattern of your breathing. That is why in yoga becoming aware of and practicing slow, rhythmic breathing is so important. Becoming attuned to your own internal metronome during your golf game is very important. It will heighten your level of inner awareness.

To experience these waves of energy flowing inside you, practice three easy steps. First, *feel the energy flowing* within you. Sense the energy circuit passing down the front of your body and up your back. Feel the energy in your spinal column. Second, *develop an intense and conscious awareness* that this energy forms the basis of every thought, emotion, and action of your golf (and life in general). Third, *breathe slowly and rhythmically* to attain total relaxation and balance. Think of yourself as a pattern of flowing energy.

Awareness of the pattern will connect you with yourself. Your golf game rides on the waves of your own creative energy. How fortunate for you that the Creator equipped you with an inner metronome. Listen to it. Use it.

THE JIGSAW PUZZLE

Let's say you're assembling an especially difficult five-hundred-piece jigsaw puzzle. Each piece has a blank side and a picture side. But there's a problem: the cover on the box is blank. Thus you don't know up front what the completed picture looks like. "No problem," you say to yourself. "I can still assemble this puzzle. Piece of cake!"

You start by placing all the pieces picture side up. At first, you're enthusiastic. Eventually, however, you get extremely discouraged and frustrated. You start to force some pieces. Assembling the puzzle is actually much more complex than you supposed. You're getting stressed out over this. You decide to seek some expert help.

Eventually, you realize that the connected and loose pieces form a familiar picture. You begin to see the picture emerge of a golfer, a golf club, and a golf course. In fact, the more pieces you connect, the more you suspect the picture is of you. You get enthusiastic about finishing the puzzle. "Sure enough," you tell yourself, "the golfer in the picture is *me*! I can't wait to complete this."

The puzzle is almost complete. You rush to insert the remaining pieces. With three pieces left, it hits you: there aren't enough pieces left to finish the puzzle! You can't believe this — a damn five-hundred-piece jigsaw puzzle missing pieces. Now what are you going to do?

You look everywhere. Maybe the missing pieces fell under the couch. Or maybe the pieces weren't in the box in the first place. Sadly, you resign yourself to accept the picture as it is — incomplete. This sad story is also applicable to golf.

Your golf puzzle, in case nobody ever told you, is not meant to be fully assembled. It will *always* have missing pieces! That's the way golf is. Accept it! And if you don't accept it, you're going to wind up in the hurt locker. Like most golfers, you have probably said this to yourself: "Today, I've finally found the *last* piece of the golf puzzle. Hurrah!"

Perhaps you fit some small piece — some small technique — into your puzzle, and it worked like a charm. But whatever piece fit today probably won't fit tomorrow. In fact, you probably forced some pieces into your puzzle. Now the pieces you forced have to come out. You're back to where you were — with an incomplete puzzle. Perhaps you need an expert to help you assemble your puzzle. You take the expert's advice, which works great on the practice range. But on the course, the expert's advice turns out worse than that meatloaf recipe your buddy Richie gave you!

Golf teases you into thinking that your game is "almost" complete. But it never is. If you're someone who demands completeness, tranquillity, and finality, don't play golf. Why? Because you'll never resolve your golf problems. Playing golf is like waging an endless and losing war. There comes a time when you must cut your losses and call a truce.

Your quest to find the missing pieces of your golf puzzle, however, is part of being human. Check this out: even my golfing friend Cliff, now in his nineties, is still making changes to his grip! He's still looking for the missing pieces. Golfers must realize that there is no finite number of missing pieces to their jigsaw puzzle. The number of missing pieces varies from round to round. There's no *final* piece.

Once you take up golf, you want to master it, conquer it, complete it. That's how the human mind operates. But when your golf puzzle — despite considerable time and effort — looks no nearer completion than it did a year ago, you stress out. Simply put, incompleteness in humans creates tension. According to researchers, incompleteness even stresses out animals. Supposedly, if you draw a partial circle on the sidewalk with some chalk and an ape wanders by and sees it, the ape will grab the chalk and complete the circle. Apparently, apes also hate incompleteness.

It's important to know how much of your golf puzzle is actually finished. Is the grip part of your puzzle complete? What about the stance part? If your picture (with no forced pieces) is nearly complete, then you can focus on the key remaining missing pieces — like your tempo or swing plane. You assemble your golf puzzle the same way you assemble a standard jigsaw puzzle: keeping the big picture in mind and taking one piece at a time. If you're not sure what pieces need to be removed or inserted, consult a golf puzzle expert — a pro.

Each puzzle piece plays a significant role. The small things — seemingly unimportant — make up the big things. For example, consider your grip and your stance. Moving your left thumb (for a right-handed golfer) clockwise a fraction of an inch on the shaft seems trivial. However, if your left thumb is improperly positioned, at impact you won't be able to rotate your forearms for added power. Also, opening your forward foot a few degrees at address seems trivial. However, if your forward foot is squared up, you may not be able to follow through properly for your one-plane swing. Big things in golf — like power and distance — are a function of little things.

John Allin, an Episcopal bishop at Trinity Church in New York, recently said, "Being head of the Church is like putting together a jigsaw puzzle while riding on a roller coaster." That description also applies to golfers, with one difference: on a golf roller coaster, you can get on, but you can't get off!

FROM GIRAFFES TO GOLFERS

All God's creatures — from giraffes to golfers — observe specific rituals. These rituals are significant. They allow us to tap into a collective memory, a shared consciousness. Rituals are congealed time.

When things are understood properly, life becomes a ritual. Rituals are the formalized things in life that get passed down, whether through teaching or instinct. Rituals are essentially time capsules. When a giraffe chews the leaves of a tree and nods its head, it taps into all other giraffes, past and present, through a collective giraffe memory.

When you perform time-honored golf rituals, you connect with all other golfers past and present. Golf's subtle and wonderful rituals form a chain stretching back to Scottish archers and fletchers who had the skills and tools to make clubs by fashioning wood and forging iron. Imagine your 6-iron having a forged-iron head, a rawhide grip, and a flexible shaft from a blackthorn bough. Imagine hitting a ball made of turned boxwood or leather-encased feathers. Imagine yourself playing on a windy and rainy Saturday in 1782 at the Royal Aberdeen.

The great rituals are heartfelt. Some anonymous golfer,

centuries and centuries ago, first viewed golf as something magical and sublime. He went out one day and greeted lovingly the course and the game. He said or did something that connected him to the richness of golf. That simple offering to golf that he repeated again and again became a ritual. That ritual was then taught and passed down. And now, many generations later, you perform the same ritual. You connect with exactly the same love of golf in exactly the same way.

The transformative experience of golf lies in its rituals: you tend the flagstick. You sling your bag over your shoulder. You insert a wooden tee in the ground. You replace a divot. You carry a lucky ball marker in your pocket. You remove a knit head cover from your driver. You caress the rawhide grip of your putter. You cringe when your putt stops an inch from the cup. You add up your score and put the card in your bag. You throw your clubs in the trunk of your car and sigh. "He who can take no great interest in what is small," John Ruskin wrote, "will take no interest in what is great."

Whatever the golf ritual might be, it's your way to express your appreciation for the game. A ritual implies that you are doing something completely and properly. You perform the ritual with a sense of passing it on. Millions of years ago someone discovered fire. Every time you strike a match or poke a stick into the open flame, you connect with the original insight of that first fire-starter. Performing a particular ritual is an expression of thanks for something special — fire, golf, or whatever. We are all connected. Rituals dramatize that connection.

Every gesture represents a connection. Your wooden tee is essentially the same wooden tee with the funnel-shaped head marketed and patented in 1922 by a New Jersey dentist named William Lowell. Calling it the Reddy Tee, Lowell popularized the tee by using an aggressive marketing campaign. He hired popular touring pros like Walter Hagen and Joe Kirkwood to publicize the Reddy Tee during tournament appearances and trick-shot exhibitions in the 1920s. That's essentially the same tee that Kirkwood used during a trick-shot exhibition in Iowa when he holed a drive of some 248 yards.

Rituals magically connect you with the legends of the game — the Hagens, Hogans, Sneads, and others — who attained a higher golf consciousness, a kind of golf enlightenment or Buddhahood.

In the East, many believe that everything ever done, ever said, and ever thought is recorded in a big book. Rituals are like a big book passed down over the years, reflecting a longing and an appreciation for common memories and experiences. Every time you pull a 5-iron from your bag, you form a connection with every golfer who has ever done the same. The way to enrich golf is to become aware of its small rituals.

GROWTH

You walk off the eighteenth green to add up your score. The math isn't pretty. This isn't the score you wanted or expected. Apparently, the lesson from the pro and the practice time on the range went for naught. In your foursome, no one played well. Maybe it was the heat. Drained and dejected, you trudge toward the clubhouse. You toss your spikes in your locker and leave. You're not sure what you need first: a cold shower or an exorcism.

As you leave, you glance back at the course. "Somewhere out there lies my golf game," you think. "I wonder if I'll ever find it again?" You spot another tired and sweaty foursome on their way to the clubhouse. Walking single file carrying their bags, they also look drained and dejected. You leave the course with low spirits and crushed hopes.

Welcome to golf's "Legion of Despair" — the army of score-oriented golfers burdened by their lofty expectations and saddened by their poor performance. You've played golf for many years, so you know the taste of disappointment. What you don't know is why you keep beating yourself up. Maybe God made golf courses, you think, so human beings have some nice place to abuse themselves. When golf makes you so miserable, how can you love it with your whole heart?

Eastern thinkers can shed some light on your misery. They attribute all suffering basically to ignorance associated with cravings and desires. They call this ignorant clinging to desires "attachment." In golf, you'll never get rid of your attachments. So don't even try! What you must do instead is become aware of them. Pay attention to what attachments are doing to you and your flow of energy. Tension, despair, and disappointment — unreleased negative energy inside you — are just forms of pain. What is pain? It's a mental and physical message saying that you're stuck. Your pain and anguish are telling you that you need to start growing.

Listen to your pain. It will help you actuate your growth. Whether it's a back pain or a golf pain, it tells you when something is wrong inside you. You may resent pain, but it will never lie to you. If you really listen to your lower-back pain, for example, it may be saying that you need a diet. Or that you're getting older. Pain will tell you many things you may not want to hear. Pain, like an old friend, will reach out to tell you this: "There's a problem inside, and you need to deal with it."

If you *really* listen to your pain, you'll reach a moment of quiet surrender. You'll finally stop struggling with your golf mess. You'll say, "I'm tired of being miserable. I want more from golf. I want to grow!"

What does growth mean? It means realizing that you are a living event. It means resolving to work through your own pain. It means being honest and courageous enough to see the whole picture and face what's going on. It means converting negative energy into positive energy.

Growth — especially golf growth — is all about awareness. In a famous article, "Concentration," Bobby Jones claimed that you'll improve only when you understand two key things: the *correct* swing and *your* swing.

Jones — whose article appeared in 1935 in *The American Golfer* — wrote, "The real road to improvement lies in gaining a working understanding of the correct swing in general, and of his swing in particular. When he does this, there will then be something on which to hang his concentration. Then he will have some chance of learning what to think about."

Growth occurs when you dig a deep hole inside yourself — through the shale and the bedrock. When you go within, you'll finally ask yourself, "What's golf telling me about myself?" and "Why am I playing golf in the first place?"

If you play golf for many years, you simply become an *experienced* golfer. However, if you learn from your many mistakes over the years, you become a *wise* golfer. Both experienced and wise golfers make mistakes. However, there's a key difference. Wise golfers — possessing the requisite awareness — learn from their mistakes. Experienced golfers don't!

There's an interesting story about a reporter who visited a monastery to interview a Zen master on his one-hundredth birthday. The reporter asked, "If you could live your life over, would you make the same mistakes?" The Zen master replied, "Yes. I would make the very same mistakes. However, I would make those mistakes *earlier*." Growth begins the moment you realize you're ignorant of what you're doing — the moment you start learning from your mistakes.

Aldous Huxley — a scientist and philosopher — believed that great knowledge and wisdom are rooted in one's desire for spiritual growth. But don't let goals and expectations limit your growth and stop your energy from flowing. When you're a beginning golfer, you need goals and expectations to direct your energy. But goals and expectations as you advance in golf can actually retard your growth. After you learn the mechanics, drop the goals and expectations. Transcend the mechanics. Rely more on feel and intuition.

Your ultimate goal is to become a devotee, an aficionado. (*Aficion* in Spanish means "passion.") You don't want to become a golf technician. You want to become a golf aficionado. You want your passion for golf to actuate your growth. Passion is the impetus for all personal growth.

Specific desires and expectations invite certain misery. Let's say your desire is to shoot in the low 80s, but it never happens. Then what? Do you keep beating yourself up? Do you keep telling yourself that you're not good enough — that you're a failure?

"So, what are you going to shoot today?" is the question you ask yourself on the first tee. The magic number in your head for today, let's say, is 84. But on the first four holes the wheels come spinning off. Unless there's a miracle, an 84 is out of the question. So — what do you do? Do you start slapping yourself with your golf glove? Do you put your golf growth on hold? Do you start thinking about tomorrow's round? Or do you adjust your desires and expectations and cut your losses?

If you desire and expect from golf only good scores, you shortchange yourself. Golf offers you so much more. If you demand only low scores from golf, you ask for so little. Why not ask golf to fill your vast human potential? Ask and you shall receive!

Here's an apt analogy. Gino, the owner of Realistic Pizza, offers you a free party-size pizza. Being the opportunist that you are, you say, "Wow, that's great. It looks delicious. But I'll take only this small piece right here." Then Gino says, "It's free! It's an extra one. It's all yours. Take it home — you can feed an army with this thing!"

But you insist on taking only one piece. You want only a fraction of the whole pizza. "Thanks anyway," you say. "I'll settle for just this one small piece." Then Gino says, "Suit yourself. But this party-size pizza is yours for the taking!"

Why take only a small piece of golf, like low scores or longer drives? Why not take all that golf affords: peace of mind, inner joy, deep contentment? Grow as a complete golfer and as a total person. Make growth your ultimate goal. Golf is one gargantuan, party-size pizza. It's there for the taking. Get on with it. We don't want to keep total growth waiting, do we?

HOW TO INCREASE
YOUR GAME'S BLOOD SUPPLY

ail Your Way to Success. Failure breeds success. In 1878, when a reporter asked Thomas Edison how he felt failing over six thousand times before he found the right filament for his lightbulb, Edison replied, "I didn't fail six thousand times. I found six thousand filaments that didn't work." If you're failure averse, you'll never grow. According to Amy Edmondson, a Harvard business professor, "Failure provides more learning in a strictly logical or technical sense than success does." Embrace failure — it's the incubator for success.

Learn the Art of Making Intelligent Mistakes. Golf gurus, including Bobby Jones, have repeated this adage: "Golf is a game played unintelligently by intelligent people." Golf growth is all about systematically eliminating your mistakes. Intelligent golfers minimize mistakes by learning lessons from their failures. Unintelligent golfers, obtuse to their failures, keep repeating the same mistakes. Stop the insanity! Start dwelling intelligently, insightfully, and reflectively on your mistakes. To bring you closer to your goals, start making *new* mistakes, *smarter* mistakes, and *better* mistakes.

Don't Operate in a Vacuum. Rely on the insights and discoveries of others. Use every golf brain in the game. Edison employed over five thousand scientists at his Menlo Park laboratory to nurture his inventions. In fact, Edison sent staff members around the globe to gather test fibers for his lightbulb filament. You don't need to invent a low-maintenance and workable golf swing. You need to select a low-maintenance and workable golf swing that some-one has already invented.

Don't Overlook the Obvious. Look at what's right in front of your nose. Let's say you've recently gained some weight. Now you don't have the flexibility you once had. So don't focus on im-proving your grip. Focus on the obvious — getting in shape. Or let's say that your swing is much too fast. Don't spend your time worrying about your swing plane. Focus on the obvious — slow-ing down your swing. (Don January was fond of saying, "Slow is long and fast is short.")

Don't Expect Shortcuts. Scientists and learning specialists — who've studied musicians, chess players, and athletes — claim that with the requisite instruction, training, and engagement, you need approximately ten years and fifty thousand hours of playing and practicing to progress from *novice* to *intermediate* to *expert* skill level. Accept that growth and improvement take hard work. (Read it for yourself in *The Cambridge Handbook of Expertise and Expert Performance*. It's all there in black and white.)

Ask, "What If?" To promote discovery and growth, keep asking "what if?" "What if" questions, once they begin, will haunt you relentlessly like mental ghosts. Asking "what if" allows you to continually tweak your golf experiments. Start tweaking. For ex-ample, asking "what if?" may help you tweak your way to dis-covering a much better way to shift your weight or release the clubhead.

Replace Certainty with Doubt. Maintaining a high degree of certainty is like being locked in a bank vault. Inside the vault, you're nice and safe. However, you can't go anywhere. So what's the point? Certainty prevents you from looking beyond the horizon for new approaches. Certainty bars you from discovering new solutions and useful alternatives. Certainty will surely poison your growth. Doubt will nourish your growth. A healthy brain needs a fresh blood supply and a fresh doubt supply. Let your doubts, hunches, and intuitions bubble up inside. Doubt invites you to pay constant attention to exactly what you're doing. The dreary road of mediocrity is paved with certainty. Somerset Maugham wrote, "Only mediocre people are always at their best."

Examine Your Past. To fix what's wrong now, reflect on what worked before. Become your golf game's resident historian. If you were putting or driving the ball better last week or last season, reflect specifically on what you were doing differently then so that you can fix what's happening now. Bobby Jones wrote, "No correction seems to have a permanent effect and as soon as our minds become busy with another part of the swing, the old defection pops up again to annoy us." Reflect on your past. Perhaps you'll discover that a subtle, simple, and inadvertent change in your setup or ball position is causing your problem.

Look for Patterns. Become aware of particular cycles, sequences, and probabilities in your game. Notice the underlying pattern of your mistakes. For example, let's say that your major screwups tend to occur toward the end of each round. Why then? Or let's say that you consistently roll your ball too far past the cup on long downhill putts or that you repeatedly chunk your sand wedge from fifty yards out. Why? Note the underlying patterns of your mistakes. Identify and target those vulnerable areas and weak skill-sets that need improvement.

Set an "Idea Quota." Edison bequeathed golfers with a wonderful success tool. He called it his "Idea Quota." Forcing himself to think creatively and act productively, Edison demanded that he create a minor invention every ten days and a major invention every six months. Edison's "Idea Quota" explains why he recorded 1,093 patents during his lifetime. After each round, lesson, practice session, videotape, golf book chapter, golf magazine article, televised golf tournament, or Golf Channel episode, vow to come up with at least one great golf idea. At the end of each golf season, vow to make at least one major breakthrough. Your mind will respond to your demands. So start demanding.

Drop Your Excuses. Stop becoming a victim of your own excuses. Excuses are big obstacles to growth. Just listen to yourself: "I don't have sufficient time to play and practice"; "I can't afford to take golf lessons"; "My sore knee doesn't permit me to pivot properly"; "I started playing golf too late in life"; "If I were as strong as Mario, I too could hit the ball far." Your excuses will paralyze your growth. Pay yourself some respect by dropping your excuses.

Think Outside the Bun. Infuse your game with ideas from disparate realms — psychology, business, physics, music, dance, history, religion, anatomy, other sports. Look for answers, solutions, explanations, theories, and applications from unexpected areas. For example, if you've studied classical ballet, relate your dance experience to golf. Apply your ballet techniques to executing a forward press or shifting your weight during the backswing. If you've ever thrown a discus, relate your track-and-field experience to developing torque in your backswing and to powerfully releasing the clubhead. If you're a great businesswoman who's turned a struggling company into a thriving success, apply your same tenacious work ethic and innovative mind-set to improving your game. Also, start to think counterintuitively. Think sideways — as well as straight ahead.

Simplify Everything. Streamline and boil down everything. Avoid cluttering your mind with complexities. Complex techniques invariably break down under pressure. Employ Occam's razor: when presented with several competing and equally valid theories, always choose the simplest theory — the one with the fewest variables. For example, if two swing theories work equally well — one containing ten steps and another containing four steps — choose the latter.

THE BIG STREAM

If you're like most golfers, you're pulled in opposite directions. You want to focus on mechanics to understand how the body executes the swing. At the same time, you want to free yourself from the tyranny of mechanics and be more intuitive. You yearn for a natural swing based on feel. So you go back and forth between the mechanical and the intuitive.

But be aware that you operate on both levels. Don't choose one or the other. Integrate both.

Reconciling the mechanical and the intuitive requires a change in perspective. Think of yourself as two streams becoming one. From one stream flows your own deep-welled emotions, intuitions, values, and goals. From the other stream flows technical knowledge, swing mechanics, and varied advice. One stream bubbles with feelings. The other bubbles with thoughts. Merge both into one big stream!

When you stand over an uphill putt, for example, your mechanical stream enables you to keep the angle of your left wrist constant, your body still, your elbows slightly bent, your eyes over the target line, your putter blade square, and your stroke a bit firm. Your intuitive stream enables you to imagine the ball dropping into the cup, to feel the softness in your hands, to establish the rhythm of your stroke, to settle your mind, to remain comfortable, to relax your muscles, to swing smoothly, and to move with oneness.

Once your two streams merge, keep them together. The big stream contains all the energy your game will ever need. Up to now maybe you've gotten by with only the mechanical stream. That stream will satisfy many of your desires and physical pleasures. But unless both streams become one, you will not find the happiness and meaning that awaits you.

GOLF BRAIN

Wouldn't it be nice to play golf like Ben Hogan or Tiger Woods right from the start? Unfortunately, that's probably impossible. However, if you can learn to focus externally — not internally — as well as Ben or Tiger, then you have a chance of playing well.

Concentration means adapting your mind to the task at hand. Tension, confusion, compulsion, anxiety, anger, indifference, boredom — the classic distractors — make concentration difficult. But when your concentration strays, you haven't actually lost it. You've just misplaced it. You've allowed some other thought to take over momentarily.

If you concentrate on too many thoughts at once, you develop "golf brain." Experiencing golf brain is like trying to concentrate on a panoramic action movie projected onto three screens simultaneously. Your brain becomes stressed and skips all over the place. You are unable to grasp, sort, and interrelate the many images coming at you all at once. Similarly, when your brain gets overloaded in golf, you can't play well. When you entertain too many scattered ideas, images, and swing thoughts, you lose concentration.

To improve your skills, cognitive psychologists recommend that you gradually employ less golf brain or internal focus (fixed control and conscious cognition) and more *golf feel* or external focus (autonomous processing). Less skilled golfers need internal focus. Internal focus takes an *intellectual* approach riveted on swing mechanics and ball striking. It tightens your muscles, restricts your flexibility, and inhibits your performance. More skilled golfers need external focus. External focus takes an *intuitive* approach fixed on ball trajectory and shot outcome. Your intuition helps you make sense of seemingly unrelated thoughts.

Your ultimate goal is to develop a state of mind in which you can intuitively sense what's most important at any moment. So take a moment to become clear about your ultimate objective. Then return to your axial theme: your tempo, your balance, your calmness, your timing. Consider all other thoughts as mere variations on that theme.

When you experience a meandering mind, anticipate the *feel* of both your swing and your shot. You should instinctively say to yourself, "Yes, this is the way golf should feel." Find an appropriate image or sensation to evoke that feel. For example, imagine the smooth, slow, languid swing of a tour pro — like Freddie Couples, who takes all the time in the world when his club is at the top. An evocative sensation or image will stay with you longer and more vividly than a thought will.

When athletes choke, invariably they say they were thinking too hard. When you choke during a meal, food gets stuck in your throat. When you choke on the course, thoughts get stuck in your brain.

THE CIRCLE

Golf is essentially about circles. You hit a round ball into a round hole for an entire round. When you play, you complete a circle, the universal symbol of unity and wholeness. Golf is a living circle. It satisfies intuitively the heart's longing for connectedness. Golf is perhaps the best reminder in sport of life's unique circular journey.

Golf weaves itself into the natural web of creation. It becomes a circle within a circle. When golf becomes a sacred encounter, you begin to confront life's two great circles: the one you live within and the one that lives within you. The purpose of being alive is to experience and appreciate both.

You can help yourself by suspending your normal patterns. Try viewing and embracing the course just once as a new and sacred circle. Try experiencing firsthand the riches around you. Try awakening to the deep rhythms that call from within.

Playing the course as a sacred circle may seem strange at first. But don't let someone else's attitude toward the game determine how you should relate to golf. When you daydream, you don't question whether you can float like a cloud. You just think of yourself floating like a cloud. Golf can become a walking dream. Turning inward, mystics claim, will bring you greater joy and peace. But how do you know that turning inward actually works unless you try it? What better place than a golf course, surrounded by incredible beauty, to turn within?

Play the course for yourself. You will grow when you dare to experiment with your own life. If you complete your circle and do not sense a shift in your spiritual well-being, then draw what you can from the experience and move on.

Imagine your round of golf as a big circle on this living earth. Wait for nature to yield quietly its gifts of insight, wisdom, and peace. Turning inward means connecting with the depths of your soul. You're more than a body and a brain playing golf. You're a soul having a golf experience. The poet Rainer Maria Rilke wrote, "The only journey is the one within."

THE RITUAL OF THE SIX GOLF TEES

Before you play your next round of golf, sit quietly and ask yourself this question: "What are the six most precious things in my life?" Think long and hard about what six things make your life wonderful. Don't prioritize them, just list them. When you're done pondering, write them down.

Next, take six golf tees from your bag, each one a slightly different color, size, or shape. Then associate each tee with a particular precious aspect of your life. For example, a red tee may represent the love of your family or a pink tee may represent your health. In the palm of your hand, hold these six frail tees. Make sure that you know exactly what each tee represents. Then put the six golf tees in your left pocket and head for the golf course.

Starting on the third hole, reach into your pocket and hold all six tees. Choose the tee representing the thing you cherish *least* of the six on your list. Put the remaining five tees back in your pocket. Then tee up the ball, hit your shot, and toss away the tee. As you work your way to the sixth tee, tap your pocket to feel the five remaining tees. Start thinking about the thing you *least* cherish that you'll have to surrender next on the sixth tee box. Do the same on the ninth, twelfth, and fifteenth tees.

By the time you reach the eighteenth tee, there will be only one tee in your left pocket — the tee representing the thing you cherish most. Tee up your ball, hit your shot, then toss away the tee. The ritual is done.

Depending on the order in which you gave up your tees, the ritual will prioritize your value system, put your life in perspective, and remind you to appreciate what you now have and what you someday won't have. This ritual, a call to go inside yourself, may not teach you any lasting lessons. (Life doesn't impart many lasting lessons.) But the ritual will give you a few small clues about how to walk your path loving what you already have.

What you learn along your path is up to you. When I performed this ritual, I learned that I needed to stop grasping for more stuff and to enjoy what I already had. I reminded myself that someday all six tees will be gone.

MEDITATION

The Chinese who practice meditation call it *wu shi*, which means "no fuss" or "nothing special." In a meditative state, your game will unfold without your having to force, manipulate, or control it.

The opposite of a meditative state is an agitated state. In that state, your mind is like a Los Angeles freeway at rush hour. Golf traffic — your swing, your score, your ego, your match, your putting — races through your mind. It's bumper-to-bumper from all directions — the past, the present, and the future. In an agitated state, your mind and body get tired fast.

In a meditative state, however, your mind is fresh and relaxed. There's very little traffic. You experience peace, silence, empty space. You are in the pure present, the immediate now. It's like removing a thick layer of dust from a mirror. You can finally see yourself clearly.

The meditative state is your natural state. You were born in that state. But when you learned the ways of the mind — how to think, to speak, to calculate — you lost touch with your inner stillness. You filled your mind with the world around you.

Your meditative state is always close by. On the course you

will no doubt be busy with other things. Amid all the noise and traffic of your mind, meditation will offer a soft whisper. But it won't stick around. It won't shout to wake you up. It will tiptoe around inside you, pausing momentarily. If you're otherwise engaged (as you probably will be), it will leave without a trace.

Unless you put your agitated mind aside, it will create more problems than you can handle. But if you slow down all the traffic in the mind, if you let thoughts and worries pass, if you let the silence arrive, if you go deep inside, meditation will happen. Have patience. Lao-Tzu called meditation "action through inaction." Tell your golf mind to wait. Meditation will show up. Meditation, in all forms, is just a method to bathe the mind.

When you learn how to enter a meditative state, you will have the feeling that you have known this state before. And you have known it before. The joy of life is in regaining it. Golf is where you can begin to do so.

THE BRIDGE

Suppose you're hitting your driver on the first tee. You tense up because you want to hit your drive long and straight. But long and straight drives won't happen without practice. It takes practice to relax your grip, stay balanced, swing slowly, bring the club back in one piece. These are the techniques you practice again — and again. And again. And again. Practice allows you to put your swing on automatic pilot.

With considerable practice, you'll resemble the tour pro who swings so smoothly you can't discern the technique. Watch pros on the practice range. They hit the ball the same way over and over. They hit the ball seemingly without having to think about anything. Their swings — effortless, powerful, and repeatable — are on automatic pilot. So where's their technique?

For them there is no technique — only pure understanding or intuition. Look at the old films of Bobby Jones, Ben Hogan, or Sam Snead. You will marvel at their languid, beautiful swings. A lot of practice on technique went into building those swings. (In fact, Hogan was the master of technique and serious practice.) The films, however, do not show the years of drudgery that made those swings possible. Practice is hard work. But it's the price you have to pay to improve. Practice yields a level of sensitivity and attunement that transcends mechanics.

You must employ technique before you can put your swing on automatic pilot. Once your swing's on automatic pilot, forget technique. You don't need it anymore. However, if you *begin* and *end* with technique, you will not progress. Technique will get in your way. You will become stuck worrying about body mechanics and dealing with tension.

When you start playing poorly, don't experiment with your swing during the round. Just keep playing. Go back to basics. Work out your problem later on the practice range. That's the place to experiment. In the East there's an apt saying: "The only truths you find on the mountaintop are the truths you bring up there." So too with golf. The only game you will find on the course is the game you bring to the course!

If you practice effectively, you will build a bridge between the mechanical and the natural. When you eventually walk over that bridge, you'll take your golf to a new level.

ACTION VERSUS ACTIVITY

Ideally, your golf should be based on action, not activity. Both are forms of doing, but their natures are opposite. The difference between activity and action reveals a key division between Western and Eastern thinking.

In the West, activity is the goal-oriented effort to become better, to transform your character. Activity is how you improve yourself. In the East, however, a goal-oriented effort to become better is a contradiction. Eastern thinkers believe you are already carrying your perfect being around with you. Therefore, you don't have to become anything. You just have to realize what's hidden within you. You are absolutely perfect as you are. In contrast, the quest for improvement focuses your attention on the future, fills you with anxiety, increases desire, and leads you down the wrong path.

From an Eastern perspective, activity is obsessive, while action is natural. Activity flows from a busy mind, action from a still mind. Activity, loaded with your past, brings restlessness into the present. Action is a natural and spontaneous response to the present. Activity is restrictive and harmful; action, constructive and beautiful.

For example, if you eat when you're not hungry, drink when you're not thirsty, or sleep when you're not tired, you're engaged in an activity. Activity means releasing your inner restlessness. Activity does not flow spontaneously. But when you eat, drink, and sleep *only* when you're hungry, thirsty, and tired — that's action.

Activity flows from the past. Whatever energy has been building up over the years becomes the activity brought to the present moment. For example, your past angers and frustrations will incorporate themselves in the activity of your swing. Although your mind will rationalize that your swing activity contains neither your past anger nor frustration, you know otherwise. An activity-based swing is tense. An action-based swing is relaxed.

In the East the image of a hollow bamboo stalk is used to suggest the empty present. If you become like the hollow bamboo, you allow infinite energy to flow into you. There will be empty space for the Divine, the Infinite, the Unknown, the Mysterious, the Powerful to enter you. The hollow bamboo is a meditation symbol for relaxation — for the mind and the body at rest.

Relaxation means the absence of activity. When time stops, that's relaxation. In relaxation the only moment is the now-moment. Don't spend your energy on the past or future. Focus on the action of the moment. Trade activity for action.

If you heard someone playing music on a bamboo flute, you might start to hum to yourself. Your humming is action. It's spontaneous. Enlightenment in golf is in knowing what is natural. When the young Zen monk asked his master to define enlightenment, the master said, "When I'm tired, I sleep. When I'm hungry, I eat." Your intuition will tell you what's natural.

WHY?

Your putt hits a spike mark and rims out. Or it strikes the flag-stick and caroms off the green. Or it overhangs the lip of the hole. Or it rolls off the green and lands in a footprint in the bunker. Or your clubhead separates from the shaft during the down-swing. Or your tee shot lands in a fairway divot hole. Why?

When you ask why in these situations, you're asking a rhetorical question. There isn't an answer. And even if there were an answer, it wouldn't help you anyway. In fact, the answer won't help at all with the matter at hand. Forget why it happened and go beyond it. You live in the present. What happened in the past is finished. Asking why gets you stuck in the past and prevents you from moving on.

In Buddhism there is a famous story about a man shot by a poison arrow. His friends summoned a doctor to remove the arrow. But the man refused to have the arrow taken out until he had a few answers. He wanted to know who shot the arrow and why. And what direction the arrow came from. And what type of wood was in the shaft of the arrow. And what kind of bird feathers gave the arrow flight.

Certainly, the man would die before he got all his answers. Buddha warned his followers about asking a lot of speculative questions. The task at hand is to remove the arrow. You need to free your mind and deal with the predicament at hand.

When you experience setbacks in your golf game, resolve to move on. A setback is an opportunity for growth. Every experience will either promote or retard your development. It's up to you to decide.

If you open your heart and mind to the energy within, you will expand your awareness. Make golf the arena in which you discover and expand your inner self. The only time you have to learn anything about your golf game is in the present moment.

If golf teaches anything, it teaches that you're not in control. First one thing happens — like your ball rolls under a willow tree — then something else happens. You have to improvise, given the situation at hand. Everything in golf is a situational surprise. (Need I remind you of the time you farted loudly and unexpectedly when you bent over to tee up your ball during the Friday night couples scramble?)

To grow means learning how to improvise, how to respond to surprises, how to manage the unexpected, how to deal with the situation at hand. The events in your game — or in your life — are not what's important. What's important is how you respond to them!

Golf consists of triumphs and setbacks. Your challenge is not to play a perfect round of golf. Instead, play to experience everything golf offers — the joy, the pain, the pleasure, the disappointment. Without pain, joy is meaningless. Never expect answers from golf — expect only the here and now. There's only one verity in golf: "Golf is what it is."

A SACRED PRAYER

Playing golf is an encounter with the unknowable, the mysterious.

With the birth of science, people started to doubt the sacred and the spiritual. But acknowledging this mystery yields a glorious conclusion: the unknown is the traditional path to the sacred.

Carl Jung based much of his theory on one key idea: that the psyche has an inherent drive toward *wholeness* and *integration*. For Jung, the psyche's attraction for the sacred was "the urge to oneness." If you play golf with your whole being, you get the feeling of being drawn toward something deeper and greater.

Few golfers ever really see the course they play on. They simply look and move on. When you "see" the course, you take it inside. You see the dew sparkle on the greens, the greenness of the fairway, the shadows at dusk. To really see the course, you need to see it with new eyes. If you knew, for example, that you'd be totally blind tomorrow, how would you view the course today?

When the light is just right on the course, the sacred moment for you will occur. It will not come as a thought or a feeling. It will not be understandable or expected. It will not lend itself to word or symbol. It will just be a fact! And what you see on the course at that moment will never be repeated. Your glance will be an extension of the mysterious.

Some theologians say that prayer is rooted in our deepest urge to unite with something larger. If that's true, then playing golf is a form of prayer. It's not so much a prayer of thanks or repentance. It's a prayer celebrating the unknowable, the mysterious, the sacred.

TREES

Most golfers view trees as bad news. Trees obstruct your line of flight, interfere with your backswing, deflect your shots, and cost you strokes. Broken limbs obscure your ball. Overhanging branches and surface roots snag your clubhead. Tree trunks make you waste shots. Leaves scattered on the fairway hide your ball. And pine needles in the rough really make for a tricky lie.

But trees can actually be your best friends. They can teach you some great golf lessons. Open up to them as you play. When you take your stance, pause momentarily and observe a tree or a stand of trees. Today, many teaching pros stress the importance of swinging flat-footed to keep a firm base. Feel your feet being rooted deeply in the earth. Become a tree. Feel its stillness, solidity, and balance. Transfer the feeling of the tree into your mind and body. The thick trunk and deep roots will anchor you. If you tend to sway or move your feet too much, a tree will teach you to stay put.

In short, *use the ground* the same way the tree does. Feel the force of the earth entering your feet and passing into your legs, hips, chest, arms, and shoulders. Gather up the power of the earth just as the tree does. "Using the ground" was Bobby Jones's expression for properly introducing the hips and legs into the shot. Just glance at the trees and remember that your power is not in your upper body. It's down below your waist.

When you swing, almost every part of your body (with the exception of your pancreas) moves. If all parts of your body moved at the same pace, speed, and direction, the golf swing would be a piece of cake. But in the golf swing, with so many moving parts, your only fixed, stable, constant element is the ground. So remember that trees are on golf courses to help you, not just to beautify the landscape. They remind you to swing flat-footed, maintain your spine angle, and keep dynamically still.

Byron Nelson used the tree metaphor to teach his pupils how to keep their heads from swaying laterally or lifting up. In *Shape Your Swing the Modern Way*, Nelson wrote, "Now, when a tree sways, what is moving? The top of the tree, not the trunk. The trunk is stationary. In the golf swing you want an action that is exactly opposite. You can move considerably underneath your head. As long as your head stays still, you can keep your balance nicely." To keep your head still, like an upside-down tree, Nelson advised his pupils to keep their legs flexed and loose and moving freely toward the target on the downswing. Imagine Nelson's image of trees standing upside down to remind yourself how to keep your head still by letting your legs below move freely toward the target.

You can also learn from trees some key emotional lessons, such as patience. Trees take a long time to grow and to spread their roots. They don't rely on shortcuts. If you expect slow and incremental growth in your golf game, you won't be frustrated or disappointed. Borrow patience from the trees around you. Expect to grow like a tree, one ring at a time.

Also, note how trees are perfectly matched to their environment. Many trees have been standing since long before you were born. Trees are in balance with the totality of nature: the earth, air, sunlight, rain, and wind. Feel, hear, and see the interconnected web of life. Feel the soft earth beneath your feet and the sun on your skin. Hear the wind through the branches. See the shadows and colors around you. Open yourself, like the branches and leaves of a tree, to the sky above. Integrate yourself to the whole course like a tree.

Trees can teach you how to swap thought for intuition. They don't intellectualize about their goals. They don't have to think about the complex biological functions they need to grow. They just take in nourishment, then actuate their potential. A tree is a living, dynamic event just like you. Become aware of the creative energy of life within you. Your energy is already inside you, so let it unfold. Depend on what's already there.

Trees can be great sports psychologists on the course, teaching you how to relax. Picture, for example, a tree in a raging storm. The small branches and leaves at the top sway violently. At the top the tree looks frail and vulnerable. However, when you consider the trunk and the roots, you realize how still and steady the tree really is.

During the storm, practice breathing in and out . . . in and out . . . in and out . . . in and out. Focus on your breathing. Inhale the stillness and steadiness of the tree. Exhale your tension. Don't wait for a storm to become the tree or to practice your breathing. Make it a habit. The trees on the course are your meditation teachers.

Trees can also help you let go of your ego. Egos thrive on comparisons! If you're playing with a much better golfer, you may become intimidated. Or if you're playing with a much worse golfer, you may become cocky. Obviously, you won't play well with either an inferiority complex or a superiority complex. Just stop making comparisons and let ego and judgment vanish. Your ego creates fiction based on needless comparisons. Remember: humans make comparisons — trees don't.

If you compare yourself with every other golfer on the course, you create a needless mental burden. As you observe the trees on the course, remind yourself to be yourself. Some trees are big and some are small. Some golfers are better than you, some worse. Who cares?

To maintain your physical and mental stability, visualize yourself as a stately oak. In fact, choose the biggest oak you can. Get in touch with it. Know that you are stronger and steadier than you suppose. Borrow from those trees their steady and quiet dignity.

You've probably never heard of Barbara McClintock. She's a noted geneticist and one of my intellectual heroes. When she died in 1992, *The New York Times* printed her obituary on the front page, a space normally reserved for fallen heads-of-state and big-time celebrities. For forty years, McClintock studied corn to figure out how genes move and carry messages.

Her biographer, Evelyn Fox Keller, asked McClintock how she did her great science. McClintock humbly replied, "Really, all I can tell you about doing great science is that you somehow have to learn how to lean into the kernel. You have to learn how to think like corn." And so too with you, Dear Golfers. To play great golf, you need to learn how to lean into the trees. Pay some respect to them. They've been giving golf lessons for years. The next time you pass a tree felled by a chain saw, strong wind, or lightning bolt on the course, express silently your condolences. One of your golf teachers is gone.

WATER

In golf, *water* is an ugly word that suggests tension, high scores, shattered confidence, puzzling rules, and, all too often, the sacrificial altar for a brand-new ball. For most golfers, *water* and *hazard* are synonymous. However, for the naturalist Henry David Thoreau, water wasn't a hazard but a reflective, deep, and fluid symbol of mindfulness. For you, water may be the golf mirror you've been looking for.

Suppose you have a shot over water. You need to use the lake or pond to your advantage. Make the water your ally. If the water is perfectly still, it reflects clearly the mountains, trees, clouds, and sky. In taking your shot, become quiet and still like the water. Bring the calmness and serenity of the surface inside your heart. Become a sparkling reflection of everything you see. The water's reflective stillness will turn you inward and melt your anxiety.

Breathe in and out, in and out. Still water is the perfect reality to quiet your nerves. Becoming still like the water, you create a solid base for insight and understanding. Calmness will create the clarity and confidence to perform the shot. When you feel the water's stillness inside you, take your shot. Use the stillness to relax you.

Identify with the water's depth. Beneath the surface ripples and waves the depths are perfectly still. Whatever colors or shadows or raindrops or leaves or breezes pass on the surface, everything below is still. Your mind is like that. When your exterior gets agitated, find the calmness below the surface. If you go deep enough in the ocean, you will be oblivious of the hurricane whipping above.

Water seeks its own level and fits any container. Take a few lessons here and adapt yourself to your circumstances. If your ball lands in a stream, just watch the water flow by. Stop momentarily and observe. Inhale and exhale naturally. Don't think about the penalty stroke. Think about how easily the water flows.

Watch the twigs and leaves float naturally in the stream. Take a lesson from the stream. Let your frustrations over a lost ball or lost stroke pass. Don't block your feelings. Label them — anger, frustration, disappointment — then move on. Let the stream wash away your feelings. Feel the flowing water inside you slowly return calmness and clarity to your mind and body. Let the water cool your anger. The stream will transform you, if you allow it. Become as adaptable and fluid as the stream.

Make the water on the course your friend. It, along with the trees, is your surest and truest guide. So stop and look into it. See an image of yourself — calm, cool, reflective, quiet.

BREAKTHROUGHS

You've been in a prolonged slump for months. Last season you were consistently breaking 90 — including a few career-low rounds of 83! Now you rarely break 100. Totally frazzled, you hit the panic button. You purchase a $399 driver, peruse instruction books, watch golf videos, hit countless range balls, and replace the St. Christopher medal in your golf bag. (You even ask your parish priest to perform an exorcism on your clubs.)

Then one evening, the club pro sees you beating balls on the range. Sensing your frustration, he stops to help you. Observing that your swing plane is too flat, he briefly explains the geometry of the swing plane. He contrasts your swing plane with the *ideal* swing plane. He demonstrates several slow-motion swings with your club. Finally, he says, "Try this: Don't hit balls for a while. Research the swing plane. Try to subconsciously program your swing by repeating it in slow motion, half speed, full speed, and blindfolded. Just take a break — you're trying too hard!"

You religiously follow the pro's advice. When you return to the course two weeks later, you feel like a new person. You're no longer stressed and unsure. Paradoxically, now you're both more relaxed and more alert. Your breathing is calm and rhythmic. Your swing, programmed into your subconscious, is smooth and effortless. Suddenly, your game returns. Whoopee! Your slump (for the time being) is over.

Admittedly, it's not all that easy. Escaping a slump requires time, effort, patience, reflection, and insight. So don't expect a free lunch. Unless you're prepared to work hard, you can't expect a breakthrough. But let's examine what researchers say about breakthroughs.

The Yerkes-Dodson Law, formulated in 1908 by Harvard psychologists Robert Yerkes and John Dodson, asserts that as stress levels increase, efficiency and performance decrease. Specifically, when your stress levels are high — as when you're grinding away on the course or practice range — your performance and efficiency decline. In sum, when you're frazzled, stop grinding.

Basing their studies on the Yerkes-Dodson Law, Harvard researchers Herbert Benson, MD, and William Proctor more recently claimed that you experience breakthroughs when you successfully balance and manage your stress. In their book *The Breakout Principle*, Benson and Proctor identify four key stages to making breakthroughs and improving performance.

First, the *struggle* stage. This is when you prepare yourself mentally and physically through exhaustive study, research, practice, reflection, and training. So do your homework by learning swing mechanics. Practice your swing without the ball, in slow motion, half speed, full speed, and blindfolded. Then practice with the ball.

Second, the *release* stage. This is when you drop your obsessive work habits. So chill out and kick back. Leave the driving range, stop banging balls, forget your golf problems, and take a walk. When you're frazzled, hitting more practice balls is counterproductive, as it increases stress. Breakthroughs occur, Benson and Proctor assert, during moments of relaxation following bouts of stress.

Shifting gears — between engaging and disengaging, working and relaxing, thinking and daydreaming — is the secret to making breakthroughs. Letting go triggers a biochemical reaction that releases increased amounts of nitric oxide in your body. According to Benson and Proctor, nitric oxide is a miraculous gas that acts as a calming agent, reversing the negative hormonal effects of stress. Nitric oxide is closely associated with lower blood pressure, heart rate, and metabolism. It opens neural pathways, allowing your brain to process new information, make connections, and on occasion, produce breakthroughs or peak experiences. Essentially, Benson and Proctor have found the body's key biochemical mechanism for reducing stress, inducing relaxation, and enhancing performance. God bless nitric oxide!

Third, the *breakout* stage. This is when you encounter new and creative ideas accompanied by a strong feeling of bliss and serenity. At this stage you encounter the unexpected, the surprising, the peak experience — like the magical yellow butterfly that lands on the toe of your golf shoe.

Finally, the *"new-normal"* stage. This is when you re-create yourself. Benson and Proctor describe an enhanced, post-breakout body-mind pattern that provides a springboard for continuous improvement, creative insights, and dramatic breakthroughs.

If you're slumping or stagnating, take a tip from Benson and Proctor: struggle, chill out, gain insights, savor peak experiences, emerge anew, and keep improving. Trust your body's natural nitric oxide relaxation response.

But advice — even from sage club pros or medical researchers — is cheap. What counts is your capacity to respond.

Too bad you can't buy portable cylinders of nitric oxide in the pro shop. Then you could keep one in your golf bag, one at work, one in your car, and one at your mother-in-law's house. (Make that two at your mother-in-law's house.)

THE FLUTE WITH NO HOLES

How many times have you heard statements like these? "If I could be a 6-handicap, I'd feel so much better." Or, "If I could hit my drives at least 240 yards, I'd be so happy." Maybe these statements reflect your sentiments as well. Underlying these statements is the idea that right now — who you are — is not enough.

Generally, the way you play golf is the way you live your life. If you're compulsive on the course, you're compulsive off the course. If you don't want your true personality to show, then don't play golf! You can't speak about golf without speaking about yourself.

You may devote your whole life to minimizing pain and maximizing pleasure. But there may be a better way to live and golf. It involves accepting both the pain and the pleasure.

There's a famous story about a young Zen monk who complains to his master.

"In the summer, I'm too hot," he says. "In the winter, I'm too cold. What should I do?"

The master replies, "Here's what you should do: in the summer, be hot. And in the winter, be cold."

This story is about acceptance. Sometimes your golf is going to be cold, sometimes hot — just accept it.

Playing golf is not about getting rid of some part of yourself and becoming something totally better. Golf is about dealing with your imperfections, which have a beauty and life of their own. Your golf game would disappear if it were perfect! Whenever something is perfect, it disappears. When the Buddha attained perfection, he disappeared and reached nirvana — which literally means "to extinguish" (like the flame of a candle).

Embrace your imperfections. Golf is about befriending who you are, just as you are. Naturally, you want to improve. But you want to improve based on knowing your whole nature, not just part of it.

There always seems to be some unfinished business in your game. A lack of consistency in your putting. A lack of distance with your driver. A lack of time to spend on your short game. A lack of work on sand shots. When your unfinished business finally gets resolved, you tell yourself that's when real golf will begin. However, one day it will dawn on you that your unfinished business *is* your game.

A famous Buddhist saying goes like this: "A flute with no holes is hard to play." It means that a flute needs a few imperfections. Without holes, the flute won't make sweet music. Everything has imperfections. And imperfections make life beautiful, especially golf.

When you accept the fact that your drives may never be long enough and your scores low enough, you'll begin to grow. Acceptance is like opening your hand. To grab a golf ball, you must first open your hand. Opening up is how you accept who you are.

Let's say someone videotapes your swing for an entire round. Later you play the tape and watch every shot. Did you cringe and tense up at all your lousy shots? Or did you calmly observe the good shots and the bad shots with total acceptance? It's important to note that acceptance doesn't mean *liking* your shots! Acceptance means gaining wisdom from your experience.

You can spend your time accepting who you are or ignoring who you are. Take your pick. Ignoring who you are will make you miserable. To grow you need to accept both sides of yourself — the good and the bad. Accept the fact that your flute has a few holes in it. Without those holes, you'll never make sweet music.

CHATTER

You and your playing partner are very different. You need silence — he needs chatter. When you three-putt, for example, you quietly leave the green. You withdraw in silence to regroup. When your partner three-putts, however, he leaves the green chattering away, oblivious as to whether you're listening.

Walking to the next tee, your partner obsessively complains about what just went wrong. The spike mark in front of the cup ...the poor follow-through stroke...the strong right hand... the steep slope of the green...the movement of the putter head ...the grip on his new Odyssey putter...the scuff on the ball... the lousy way the grass was mowed...the position of the hole ...the shadow on the green...the distracting noise from the adjoining fairway...the hole liner sticking up...the worm just outside his line...the uneven roll of the ball...the number of unfixed divot marks...the chronic lower-back problem...the way Tiger always lines up his putts...and the mushroom pizza last night from Realistic Pizza with practically no cheese on it (even though he told Gino he wanted extra cheese).

The official rules of golf say nothing about chatter. Section 1, on etiquette, basically offers commonsense advice ("No one

112

should move, talk or stand close to or directly behind the ball or the hole when a player is addressing the ball or making a stroke"). The rules of etiquette, based largely on courtesy, are unwritten, unspecific, and problematic.

How many times on the first tee has muffled chatter gotten under your skin? It's considered a breach of etiquette to talk when someone is addressing the ball or swinging. But few golfers consider it a breach of etiquette to talk your ear off as you walk. Right? As far as they're concerned, they're just being sociable. If chattering incessantly on the golf course were a punishable crime, thousands of golfers would be behind bars.

Golfers chatter to avoid silence. Golf chatterers are not really talking to anybody. Having some poor victim nearby gives them an excuse to chatter. (Golf chatterers, however, generally are quiet when they're alone in public. They've seen how those who chatter madly to themselves at malls and bus terminals get taken to the hospital.)

If you're polite or thick-skinned, you'll pretend to listen and perhaps offer an occasional nod. All that time, however, the chatterer is stealing your priceless peace of mind and assaulting your tranquillity.

Chatter is a form of catharsis, a coping mechanism for stress. Through chatter, golfers are essentially cleansing away their stress. Cleansing yourself is admirable. But don't throw your dirt on somebody else. Cleanse yourself privately. After you change the oil in your truck, for example, you don't wipe your filthy hands on someone's clean shirt or dump your blackened oil down the sewer grate (at least I hope you don't). Chattering simply transfers your "dirt" to others who are obliged to listen.

Chatter flows from inner tension. Silence flows from inner peace. Golf isn't a walking monologue; it's a walking meditation. And the basis of all meditation is stillness. Meditative stillness is achieved by putting gaps between your thoughts and breaths. Chatter removes all the mental gaps you need for awareness and clarity.

Chatter stops you from going within to solve your problems. The Eastern way of solving problems is through meditation. Meditation, a form of relaxation, involves going deeply and quietly within. Conversely, the Western way of solving problems is through analysis. Analysis, a form of thinking, involves bringing buried things to the surface to face them openly.

Analysis — a form of horizontal mental energy — is like swimming. Swimming is done on the surface. Meditation — a form of vertical mental energy — is like diving. Diving is done below the surface. The problem with chatter is that it blocks your vertical energy. Listening to interminable chatter, you can't dive deeply to the stillness at your center.

I'm not saying you should become a mute on the golf course. Golf is a social and communal activity. It's important to converse with your playing partners. What I'm saying is that for everyone's sake, you need to walk the middle path. Be neither too silent nor too talkative. If you stray, however, stray toward the path of silence. Silence carries tremendous force and energy.

If you walk closer to the path of silence, your words and thoughts become more significant. Periodic gaps of silence in your conversation make your words and gestures more meaningful. Silence is the source of all energy.

Walking a path of relative silence is like playing a single note on a piano in a hushed room. The note reverberates profoundly because of the silence on either side of it. A typical Japanese painting, with only a few bamboo stalks, or a typical Japanese haiku, with only seventeen syllables, evokes composure through the open space of canvas or page. Walking a path of relative silence is the key to composure.

THE EMPTY BOAT

Let's say you just had a career round. You fired an 84 under tough conditions. To celebrate, you stop in the clubhouse for a drink at the bar. You immediately run into tipsy Roland, who says, "Hey, how ya doin'? Broken 100 yet?" You remain cordial but reserved. You nod affirmatively and walk away. The comment strikes you like a thunderbolt. Your mood suddenly changes. A moment ago you were buoyant. Now you're miffed about an offhand comment. It dims the glow in your heart.

The point of this story is not about the person who made the flip remark. The point is about your reaction. Why would you allow someone to dictate how you feel about yourself, to destroy your peace of mind?

It's like this. If you see a drawing of a ham sandwich on a menu, you know the ham sandwich is only a representation, right? It's a picture of someone's reality of a ham sandwich. It's an idea without substance. You can't eat the picture of the ham sandwich. It won't satisfy your hunger or nourish you. But when you foolishly confuse representations of ham sandwiches with real ham sandwiches, you invite suffering. It's the same with someone's crass comments. Why get irritated over someone's false picture or stupid appraisal of you?

In his parable of the empty boat, Chuang-Tzu says that the perfect person is like an empty boat. In the parable a man was crossing a river when an empty boat collided with his own skiff. But the ill-tempered man couldn't get angry with an empty boat. He could get angry only if he saw a man in the boat. Had he seen a man in the boat coming toward him, the ill-tempered man would have shouted repeatedly and cursed at him to steer clear. But the ill-tempered man couldn't get angry at an empty boat.

The parable is about throwing out whatever you find in your boat until it's empty. Toss out your anger, fear, jealousy, pain, pride until you are totally empty. When you are empty, then you are full. When your boat is empty there will be no conflict, no anger, no hurt. If your boat is empty, you will find the peace of mind you've been looking for. For Chuang-Tzu the most worthy trait is egolessness. Everything else follows.

If you remain an open boat, no one can manipulate you. There is a famous story that illustrates this key point. One day the Buddha was walking through a village where people met him with insults and rudeness. As the people hurled their profanities at him, the Buddha simply listened attentively and politely. Then he calmly said, "Thank you for coming to meet me. Unfortunately, I'm in a big hurry as I have to walk many miles to the next village. People are waiting for me there. So I can't spend any more time with you now. Please excuse me. However, if you have more insults to heap on me, please save them. I will be passing through your village tomorrow afternoon. Then you can finish insulting me. But for now, kindly excuse me."

The people in the village couldn't believe their ears. They were amazed at the Buddha's serene nature. Then one villager asked the Buddha, "Didn't you hear our insults? Are you deaf, man? We've been insulting and abusing you — yet you've uttered not a word in response."

Then the Buddha said something like, "Guys, if you wanted to get a rise out of me, you're ten years too late! Ten years ago, I would have reacted. Not now. Then I was a slave. Now I am my own master. Today I refuse to let others manipulate me. I act according to myself, not according to anyone else. I act according to my own inner needs. You felt a need to insult and abuse me — that's fine. So you insulted and abused me. You had your fun. That's fine by me. I hope you fulfilled your inner need. My inner needs, however, are very different from yours. As far as I'm concerned, your insults and abuse are meaningless because I don't *accept* them."

If you accept the insults of others, you're obliged to react. But if you remain totally detached, what can someone do? You can't be manipulated. If you're conscious — aware of the situation and your inner needs — you'll *act* calmly. If you're unconscious — unaware of the situation and your inner needs — you'll *react* harshly. It's up to you.

Golf speaks to the ego. That's why most golfers are filled boats. Filled with ego, golfers tend to get angry and miserable. When you empty your boat and cease making distinctions, your ego will vanish and your contentment will appear. Step up to the bar at the 19th Hole and celebrate gleefully your low round. Given a choice between swallowing someone's insults or an ice-cold beer, always choose the beer!

THE NOW-MOMENT

When you open the present moment, it contains everything you need. Now is the only moment you can be sure of. It holds the miraculous and mysterious reality of your existence. So if you take good care of the present moment, you won't have to worry about what is going to happen next.

The now-moment implies a profoundly different sense of time when you're on the course. Suppose you hit a 250-yard drive down the center. You're elated. You can't wait to hit your next shot. You quicken your walk. Your heart starts to beat faster. You're pumped. You arrive at your ball. You wait. You anxiously remove a club from your bag. Your hands feel sweaty. You can't wait for your playing partners to hit their shots. Then it's your turn to play.

You take a few practice swings. You tense up. You leap into the future by imagining a possible birdie on this difficult hole. You imagine what your score will look like after this hole. You swing. But you swing too fast, too hard. You hit rather than swing. You yank the ball hard left. You ignored the now-moment that contained the shot.

The now-moment is never forced. Your shot happens at a specific now-moment. It doesn't happen any sooner or any later.

It happens when it happens. Don't slow down or speed up any-thing — your walk, your swing, your breathing. The now-moment occurs exactly when it's supposed to occur. Don't rush to the ball . . . to the tee . . . to the green . . . to the clubhouse. "Hasten slowly" — that's what monks say.

Being aware of your breath is the best way to become fully present. Breathe through your nose. Become conscious of slow-ing down your breathing. Synchronize your breathing and your walking. Walk slowly the way tour pros walk. Count your ex-hales in sets of five. Don't rush. You don't want to miss your ap-pointment with the now-moment.

In the now-moment, flow with whatever happens. Feel your mind flow through your entire body. Think with your whole body. Feel your swing being relaxed and effortless. Let the club-head naturally gather up the ball and send it skyward. Don't hit the ball — simply swing the club and *invite your ball to fly*!

Enjoy walking to your ball. Fill each now-moment with won-der and joy. The real miracle isn't walking on water; it's walking on the golf course.

Some Asian villages have a beautiful custom to remind everyone to stay in the present moment. Without warning, a spe-cial bell sounds in the center of the village. Everyone stops for a moment. They pause to contemplate the here and now. They turn inward. The bell reminds them to become more awake, more alive, more mindful of the present moment.

On the golf course, you can do the same thing. Imagine a bell sounding. Pause for a few seconds. Drop all your personal and emotional baggage. Feel your body. Ground yourself in the present moment and become more awake.

Take good care of the present moment. Live there. It's where you'll find yourself, where golf growth resides. Forget moments lost or yet to be. You have only this moment.

BEGINNER'S MIND

Robert Oppenheimer, the famous nuclear physicist, once observed some kids playing outside his laboratory window. Those kids, he told a friend, could solve his toughest physics problems because they creatively perceive the world in ways he no longer could. To solve your golf problems, try to perceive the world as a child.

A childlike mind is open to freshness and wonder. A child has "beginner's mind," a mind ready and available to see things for the first time. That's why a child finds richness and magic in each ordinary moment.

In the West an empty mind is synonymous with being vacuous and stupid. In the East an empty mind is a ready and receptive mind. Emptiness makes existence and growth possible.

This point is illustrated in a famous story. A noted Zen master received a visit from a learned professor who wanted to know about Zen. The master served tea. He filled his visitor's cup and kept on pouring. The tea overflowed and spilled on the floor. Finally, the professor exclaimed, "The cup is overfull. No more will go in!" The master responded, "Like this cup, you are full of your own opinions and assumptions. How can you learn about Zen unless you first empty your cup?"

Shoshin (beginner's mind) is a famous Japanese term. It denotes being empty, receptive, ready, and free. It suggests a mind available to entertain new possibilities. Beginner's mind means that you are ready to accept, to doubt, to weigh many possibilities. When you adopt a beginner's mind, you embrace the potential for real golf growth.

Let go of your rigid beliefs about the right way or the best way. The right way or best way is only an illusion of control and security. Avoid the egotistical rut of thinking that you know more than you do. Surrender to the many mysterious ways of golf. Admittedly, all of us fear change and the unknown. But if you embrace what Native Americans call "the great mystery," you will discover your wholeness.

Empty your golf mind of desires and expectations. Attachment to desires and expectations will sour you. How many times in golf do you get what you expect? Your beginner's mind won't have numerous cravings, won't make heavy demands, and won't limit you. When you have no thoughts of achievement or self, you stand to learn something.

Luke 18:17 says: "Whosoever shall not receive the kingdom of God as a little child shall in no way enter Heaven." It's the same thing for the Kingdom of Golf: "Whosoever shall not play golf with the mind of a child shall in no way enter golf Heaven." If your golf cup is too full, empty it.

MINDFULNESS

The practice of mindfulness brings the mind back home. Once an old woman asked the Buddha how she could become enlightened. The Buddha told her to become aware of every movement in her hands, for example, when she drew the water from her well. By becoming mindful of her hands, she would achieve a meditative state of calmness and alertness.

If you begin with a mindful awareness of each movement of your hands, you'll stay calm and controlled. Eventually, this awareness will become the intuitive feeling of your swing. Your hands are the body's connection between the mind and the club.

Keep your mind totally in tune with your body. If your mind "exits" your body, you are no longer mindful. You're distracted or anxious about something else. Consider the time you spend on distraction and anxiety. If you spend even a fraction of that time on mindfulness, you will clear your golf mind.

When you bring mindfulness to golf, you unite the elements of body, mind, and environment. Golf suddenly becomes a rhythmic dance. The more you practice, the more mindfulness will become effortless, simple, and natural. It will happen by itself. When you hit a golf ball or wash a dish, do so mindfully. Wisdom doesn't come from any specific object. It comes from a deep and penetrating awareness of experiencing who you are.

There is a wonderful story about being fully awake. Soon after the Buddha became enlightened, he passed a man cutting trees in the forest. The man was amazed at the radiance of the Buddha. The man said, "My friend, what are you? Are you a god? Are you an angel?

"No," said the Buddha.

The man asked, "Well, then, are you a magician or a wizard?"

Again the Buddha answered, "No."

The man then asked, "Are you a man?"

The Buddha replied, "No."

"Then, my friend, what are you?" the man asked.

The Buddha simply replied, "I am awake!"

When you play golf mindfully, you too will radiate. One day someone may ask you, "Are you a spirit, a yogi, a pro, a golf wizard, or a human being?" Tell them, "No, I am awake!"

Once a monk complained to the Buddha about not being able to remember the two hundred or so rules for being a monk.

The Buddha said, "Well, can you remember *one* rule?"

The monk said he could.

The Buddha replied, "Be mindful!"

Everything else flows out of that awareness. So too with you. Can you remember one rule to improve your game? Be mindful!

THE TWO PATHS

There are two paths in golf: the one you follow and the one you blaze. You should walk both paths. In golf, you continually make and remake, program and deprogram yourself by walking two paths.

The path you follow is someone else's. There's nothing wrong with that. You travel someone else's path when you take lessons, model others, read books, and watch videos. The path you follow is a glorious path. Consider, for example, walking the path recorded in books by such legends as Ernest Jones, Percy Boomer, Bobby Jones, Ben Hogan, Sam Snead, Jack Nicklaus, and Tiger Woods. A golf book written by a legend is a rare luxury. It will allow you to walk along with Bobby Jones as he shares with you his collective knowledge and wisdom. It's important to learn what the legends can teach you.

To follow the path of another requires the right mind-set, teacher, and occasion. Without the right mind-set, you will learn nothing — even from the greatest teachers. The analogy of the four pots illustrates the key problems associated with a golfer's poor mind-set. The first pot, with a hole in the bottom, represents the *unteachable* golfer. This golfer lacks the aptitude or desire to grasp and retain the lesson. Regardless of its merit, the lesson leaks out. The second pot, full of poison, represents the *judgmental* golfer, who distorts or resents learning from others. Everything becomes bitter and tainted. The third pot, turned upside down, represents the *distracted* golfer, who is asleep or unmotivated. The fourth pot, filled to the brim, represents the *know-it-all* golfer, who already "knows" everything.

Walking someone else's path means trusting someone else's truths. But there are times when you must walk your own path. Making your own path can be both a joy and a frustration. Walking your own path means daring to experiment with your life.

Trade control for discipline. Control and discipline are opposites. Control means being forced, reactive, dogmatic, and unnatural. Discipline, on the other hand, means being free, spontaneous, and natural. *Discipline* and *disciple* come from the same root, which means "to learn." A disciple is simply someone ready to learn. A disciplined person is someone with the requisite readiness and openness to learn.

Don't become a *student* of golf — become a *disciple* of golf. But don't become a slavish disciple of any golfer, no matter how great that golfer is. Become a golf disciple by developing your own understanding and by walking your own path. When you're on your own path, your bliss will flow.

The Buddha once remarked, "If you see the Buddha on the road, kill the Buddha." This odd statement simply means: "Be your own person!" The Buddha advised his followers not to accept his truths or teachings. He urged his followers to accept only the things they experienced as true. And so with you. Walk two paths: yours and those of others. If you — as many golfers do — walk only someone else's path, you'll compromise your sense of wonder.

When you go on a nature walk, you may follow the main

trail for a while. But, at times, you may want to leave that trail to explore things for yourself. In learning golf, you need to both follow the main trail and make your own trail. You may want to deviate from the trail long enough to experiment with something different. How about Moe Norman's *Natural Golf*? Try it. See what happens. Maybe you'll develop a hybrid form of "natural golf" that works great for you.

Trust others and yourself. Your goal and birthright is to become yourself, not Annika Sörenstam or Tiger Woods. What works for them may not work for you. Annika's or Tiger's golf shoes probably won't fit you. Test things for yourself. Accept some things and reject others. Take the golf that's best for you. Consider Basho's advice: "Do not seek to follow the footsteps of the men of old — seek what they sought."

ACCEPTANCE

Acceptance won't happen all by itself. Don't be surprised if you experience periods of anger and denial before you arrive at acceptance. When those periods pass, start to cultivate acceptance. Spend your energy on acceptance. Don't waste it on anger and denial. Acceptance involves developing the willingness and awareness to see things as they are. Anger and denial, fed by fear and desire, will cloud your mind. Acceptance, on the other hand, gives you the clarity, honesty, and conviction to grow.

Here's a little story to illustrate what acceptance is all about. Let's say a swarm of crickets chirp outside your bedroom window all night long. How are you supposed to sleep? The racket is driving you nuts. You issue a condition: you won't sleep a wink until those crickets stop chirping! Tossing and turning in bed, you fight the noise outside your window. You put a pillow over your head and stuff cotton in your ears. You keep asking yourself, "When are these stupid creatures going to shut up and give me a break?"

But the problem is not the crickets. The problem is *fighting* the crickets. As soon as you rescind your condition, as soon as you stop fighting and accept the situation for exactly what it is

— a noisy and miserable summer night — you'll finally get some sleep.

Acceptance is a type of mental reprogramming. It allows you to unblock your energy flow and cope with the situation. In time the cricket noise will become a lullaby. You'll enjoy their melodious sound. Finally, you won't be able to fall asleep without the crickets outside your window.

A bad golf day has no meaning in itself. The only way a bad golf day means anything is in relation to a good golf day. Expect, accept, and embrace golf's good and bad sides. In fact, get down on your knees and thank the Almighty for your bad golf days.

Your good golf days will teach you things. But your bad golf days will teach you far more. Bad rounds, if you openly accept them, contain a wealth of hidden forces and possibilities. Every three-putt, every shank, every hooked drive is a seed of potential personal growth. What you do with your seeds is up to you. You can toss away your seeds in anger or pretend they don't exist. Or you can plant, nourish, and protect them and watch them grow. If you plant and nurture watermelon seeds, watermelons grow. If you plant and nurture golf seeds, golf grows.

STANDING STILL

If golf creates in you a state of chronic anxiety, why play? Why shell out big bucks — for the dues, fees, carts, and titanium drivers — to torment yourself? It's like paying for the opportunity to stroll through a minefield or to get shot at. Why spend time and money to beat yourself up? Only masochists punish themselves the way golfers do.

Even on rainy days, golfers punish themselves because they can't go out and punish themselves. Can you imagine people getting stressed out over the fact that they can't get stressed out? Stressed-out golfers on rainy days are like caffeine addicts who wake up one morning to realize there's no coffee in the house! The anxiety of not having the caffeine (or golf) is worse than the anxiety that caffeine (or golf) itself creates. The good news, however, is that there are tested and true techniques to relieve golf stress.

You may think that meditation is only for yogis and weirdos. Not so! Meditation is a timeless and effective technique for relaxation and mental self-control. If you have time to breathe, you have time to meditate.

In meditation there are four postures: sitting, standing, walking, and lying down. The first three postures are ideal for golf. (However, don't dismiss lying down. Many times I've stretched out on the grass to wait calmly for a slow group ahead to play out.)

Most of the time during a round of golf you just stand around. So learning standing meditation is important. You breathe when you walk. You breathe when you stand. So before you hit a critical shot or take a crucial putt, rely on standing meditation to relax and center you.

Trees are living practitioners of standing meditation. There is power in stillness. Giant oaks and small saplings stand still and erect, yet continue to grow. North American sequoias grow for thousands of years, and so do ginkgo trees in China. Trees are the oldest living things. They must know something we don't. Trees just stand still. If you stand still, you'll become more relaxed, refreshed, and focused.

Standing meditation is simple. Go off by yourself and just stand calmly and quietly. Keep your back fairly straight. Put your feet out at a 45-degree angle. Bend your knees just slightly. Keep your eyes half closed. Rest your tongue on your upper palate. Close your mouth. Breathe through your nose. Take in deep abdominal breaths. Fill your belly with air.

Feel your feet on the earth. Imagine your breath drawing in energy through the soles of your feet. Circulate this energy through your body. Draw in relaxation and calm energy. Let out tension. As you exhale through your nose, smile gently. (Smiling will alleviate your tension.) Feel the air go in and out of your nostrils. Smile.

A fetus in the womb breathes from its lower abdomen through the umbilical cord. Only at birth do infants start to use their lungs. Nonetheless, infants still use their lower abdomen to breathe. By breathing abdominally, infants gain an active and flowing supply of energy that promotes rapid development. In the East, they call this flow of body energy *chi*.

As you age, your breathing localizes in your upper chest. You forget how to breathe through your belly. This restricts the amount of oxygen entering your body. "The perfect man," said Chuang-Tzu, "breathes through his heels, while the ordinary man breathes through his throat."

Stand calmly and become aware of your breathing. That's all. Avoid all thoughts and anxieties. Don't think about your next shot. It's too early for that. Try to create a gap between your previous thought and your next thought. Make the gap as wide as possible. When thoughts pop up in your mind, return calmly to patterned breathing. Feel your belly and chest expanding and contracting. Feel your pulse. Realize that the aim of meditation is to achieve a state of being, not doing.

Scan your body for tensions. If there is tension in your back or jaw or shoulder, ask yourself, "What does it feel like?" Bring these tensions into the open. Identify with the tension. If you feel tension in your stomach, place your hands on your stomach. Imagine that your hands are magnets, pulling out the tensions as you inhale. As you exhale, feel your stomach contract. Feel your hands removing the tension. Imagine hot waves of tension leaving your stomach. When the tension passes, drop your hands to your side.

Let the surroundings enter you. Keep your eyes half closed. Let a specific object choose you. Take on the soft, gentle quality of everything around you. Feel the flow of energy inside you. Hold your club gently or not at all. Drink in everything. Unify the whole scene — the green grass, white ball, and blue sky.

Don't do — just be. Bring the mind into its own natural state. Move into a state of relaxed awareness. When your mind is calm and focused, your body movements become one. Standing meditation will bring your mind home.

THE GOLF GODS

Golfers often invoke the golf gods — the alleged dispensers of good and bad fortune. The golf gods will bless and torment you. Like when your crucial, "gotta have it" four-foot putt rims the cup and plops in! "Whew! Thank you, God! I needed that putt." Or when your 5-iron from 185 yards away lands in the greenside bunker, failing to carry the trap by one inch. Instead of being pin high on the green, you're buried. "Can you believe that? One lousy inch!" Looking heavenward, you curse the gods.

The golf gods hear only certain prayers. They don't reward or punish you. That's not their job. A golf prayer is a monologue directed to the open sky. The golf prayer is its own immediate reward. It's not for something in the future. If your golf prayers are for all the things you need during your round, your prayers are for naught. Don't pray out of greed or fear.

Pray to the golf gods to express your joy. Those are prayers of affirmation. Those are the prayers that golf gods love. Pray whether there are golf gods or not. The golf gods are only a device to help you express your joy. Once you learn how to pray on the course, forget about the golf gods. Your prayer is enough in itself.

If you love to sing, you don't ask if there's anyone around to hear you. You don't sing because some cosmic being in the sky loves to hear you sing. Singing is reward enough. You love singing. And that's it! Singing opens your heart and mind. So too with saying your golf prayers. They express your joy for this great game.

Feel the sky above. Feel the warm earth below you. Merge yourself with sky and earth. Sense the energy of nature all around you. Let your body vibrate with energy. Let whatever happens happen. Acknowledging your joy is the golf prayer. It's not an activity but a state of mind.

Your prayers won't sway the golf gods to help you win a match. If you pray and your opponent doesn't, don't expect special favors. Expect instead a flow of energy. Expressing your golf joy, you surround yourself with positive energy. It's a way of becoming more receptive, of opening yourself to the beauty around you.

Golf prayers acknowledge the sacred and infinite wonder of the game. When your love for the physical intensifies, you enter the metaphysical. The golf gods don't dispense golf luck. They dispense golf joy. When you become thankful for the golf joy that fills you with wonder, the golf gods will listen.

You may have a thousand golf prayers for a thousand things. The golf gods have only one: "Do not be indifferent — to this day, to each other, to this game!"

LISTEN

Listen to the sounds of golf as if you were listening to music. The swish of an iron through freshly cut grass. The thwack of a titanium driver. The clink and clank of clubs in the bag. The rattle of the ball rolling around the metal cup liner. The thud of the flagstick dropped on the green. The plink of the putter head. The faint click of wooden tees in your pocket. The plop of raindrops on the umbrella. The squish of shoes on the wet fairway. The rustle of branches in late afternoon. The chirps of spring robins. The honking of migrating geese overhead. Just listen for a moment. Stop the world and open each dynamic and available moment.

Practice listening as if you were a monk connecting the physical and the spiritual. Don't do anything. Just be receptive. Keep your ears open. Listen intently. Cheerfully. Even if the sounds don't seem worth listening to. The sounds will become a form of music. They will energize you in the same way music energizes you.

Listening will also expand your consciousness. When you train yourself to listen carefully, you adopt the frequency range similar to that of a gong. It's like this. Put two gongs in a room.

When you strike one gong, the other will start to vibrate. Gongs, sharing the same frequencies, respond in sympathetic resonance to the sounds around them. All gongs have a unique range of frequencies. Vibrate one gong and you vibrate both.

The same is true with you. Sound makes up a big part of your golfing reality. Sound is a form of energy. Listening to the sounds of golf is a form of meditation, of increasing your awareness. For example, when you resonate to the sound of your metal driver connecting solidly, you attain a sense of enormous power. Listening meditation expands and empowers you. Awaken to golf sounds and you will resonate like a gong.

To develop a higher degree of awareness, monks in the Himalayas practice listening meditation. They listen in on sound energy that stretches from the earth to the stars. The monks resonate to the sounds of the cosmos. Inner and outer frequencies converge. Two gongs become one. The monks gain a sense of their own immensity. Listening meditation opens you.

Listening meditation is not a listening to or a listening for, but a *listening in*. You enter the sound. The sound enters you. The two merge like the raindrop and the ocean. The raindrop merges with the ocean. The ocean merges with the raindrop. It's the same thing. Certain golf sounds, like the whoosh of the perfect swing, awaken in you latent feelings. Don't try to understand the feelings. Just let the sounds stir you.

If golf is purely physical, you miss the splendor and mystery of the game. As a purely physical activity, golf fills only half your needs. Only when golf becomes metaphysical will you connect with something larger and satisfy your deep longing. Care about *how* you play. But also care about *why* you play!

According to Hindu legend, Shiva invented an instrument called a rudra vina. It was made of gourds, animal guts, animal horns, and anything else he could find. The instrument made magical sounds. It connected the listener with the music of the universe.

The ancient Scots invented some instruments, too. They were made of wood, leather, and feathers — a golf club and a golf ball. These instruments made magical sounds that connected the listener to the music of the universe. Listen to the symphony of the course. Listen to golf instruments you carry. Listen carefully to the music of golf. Then resonate like a gong.

THE DANCE

You are playing alone at dusk. The pastel clouds steal across the heavens. Shadows, chasing one another, cover the fairway. The light wind is a distant sigh. The sun floats toward the horizon. You calmly stand beside your ball. You are filled with a rush of perfect happiness. The rush of time. The end of day. Now the world seems so strange, so common, so wonderful. Is there a golfing moment more precious, more golden?

During such moments, you and golf become one. Golf suddenly takes on a whole new quality. Seemingly you walk the course for the first time. You experience a mystical feeling that you can't express. You are transformed, purified, possessed. You play as if you were in love with the universe. No longer is golf just a healthy and wonderful exercise. Golf is now a dance with your lover.

Moments of golf ecstasy turn into a divine dance. The dancers disappear into the dance. They lose themselves in the joy of dancing. They reach a point of transcendence and liberation — releasing the ego, the intellect, the tension. The body, no longer hindered by its own self-conscious movements, dances freely.

Dancers, so totally involved in their dance, make no distinction between themselves and their actions. The doer and doing merge.

When you remove the distinction between golfer and golfing, you unify mind and body, subject and object. However, if you stand aside and critically and objectively watch yourself play golf, you and golf will never merge. Participate and lose yourself in the dance.

How you do it is irrelevant. Just do it. Let golf flow in its own way. Let the union happen on its own. Golf is both *doing* and *being*. Relinquish conscious control. Golf is simply playing. Never forget that. When you let the energy flow through your body, as if you were dancing, golf will happen naturally and intuitively.

When you are dancing, do you analyze every movement your body makes? Obviously not! You may practice certain dance routines and steps. But when you dance, you just dance. If you try to observe and critique yourself during the dance, you become too wooden and self-conscious. Your body becomes an encumbrance. Dancing becomes an uncomfortable exercise.

Golf is rhythmic play. It's not an intellectual exercise like trying to solve a physics problem. Golf is a biorhythmic dance. You can tap into the same biological rhythms and muscle memories in golf that you would in dance. Free up and trust your body to perform the instinctive movements that golf demands. The key to golf is a smooth and graceful swing. Both a smooth and graceful swing and a dance are developed through feel. And feel is guided by intuition, not by conscious and rigid control.

When you practice dance or golf, concern yourself with technique. However, when you finally get to dance, rely on the body's instinctive wisdom. Learn how to let go. Learn how to forget technique. Trust your muscle memory. Zen masters, judo instructors, hatha yoga teachers, and others who stress the unity of body and mind suggest that Westerners have lost touch with their body's wisdom. Westerners have become too cerebral for their own good!

Would you dance if someone stood there and evaluated you? I doubt it. In golf, no one evaluates your swing any more critically than you do.

Make your golf swing a waltz and work on your rhythm. A good, slow waltz rhythm will diffuse tension (especially in the hands and shoulders), quicken the clubhead, and improve your timing and pace. Become a dancer-golfer and concentrate on your footwork. Use your legs and swing from the ground up. Going back, start your swing by rolling to the inside of your left foot and turning your left knee to shift your weight. (Think of your weight shift as a coiling motion rather than a sliding motion.) Let your waltzing footwork in turn move your hips and shoulders in unison. Rely more on *the subconscious feel* and less on *the conscious think* of your swing. Diffuse your energy through your entire body. Stay in waltz time.

Remember, too, that dancers are artists. Dancers don't over-intellectualize. They listen to their body rhythms and become one with their movements. Practicing mechanics and techniques, they program their muscles to react automatically. Purging all thoughts and feelings, dancers attempt to lose themselves in their dance.

Golf is a natural and liberating dance. Unless you let go of your body, you will never discover your instinctive and supple grace. A century ago in China, Master Kano — a martial arts practitioner — realized the importance of this essential principle. He observed that despite their apparent strength and thickness, the branches of a snow-covered fir tree cracked after an ice storm. Then he noticed something curious. The neighboring marsh reeds, so frail yet so pliable, survived the storm unharmed.

He concluded that the supple and nonresistant nature of the marsh reeds allowed them to dance fluidly and naturally. The dancing marsh reeds rode out the storm undamaged. From this observation, Master Kano derived principles of modern judo.

Let your body — supple and nonresistant — dance to the energy that flows within. Flow with that energy. The whole mystery of golf is in the divine dance. When you learn to dance, golf becomes so clear, so natural, so simple.

NO MIND, RIGHT MIND

Your practice swing feels fluid and rhythmic. But your actual swing, moments later, feels forced. Why? The answer to this vexing question can be found in the most unlikely place. Three centuries ago, a Japanese Zen master named Takuan wrote a remarkable letter to a famous shogun swordsman. The letter, explaining the relationship between Zen and swordsmanship, contains the answer to our question. Takuan's letter emphasizes the concept of *mushin*, or "no mind."

Mushin is the essence of martial arts. It denotes a state of mind in which practitioners rid themselves of their inhibitions and egos. They practice mechanics. But they practice without judging everything as good or bad, success or failure.

Mushin corresponds to your unconscious state. To wield a sword or swing a golf club effectively, you essentially become an automaton. That is, you become consciously unconscious or unconsciously conscious — take your choice! You let your mind flow freely throughout your whole body. In your practice swing, your mind flows freely. In your actual swing, your mind stops. That's the difference.

In either swordsmanship or golf, if you "stop" or "localize" your mind, you will be in the hurt locker. So where do you "put" your mind when you play golf? In your swing? Your hands? Your club? Your feet? Your ball?

Actually, you don't put it anywhere. You put it everywhere! Because wherever you put your mind, you stop or localize it. And stopping the mind represents a form of delusion.

Suppose you're looking at an apple tree. If you look at a single red apple, you will not see the other apples nor will you see the whole tree. You will see only that one apple. However, when you look at the tree with nothing in mind, you will see everything. By focusing narrowly on a single apple, you miss seeing other apples, the branches, the trunk, the whole tree, the clouds, the sun, and the sky.

If you focus on your hands, only your hands will absorb your mind. If you focus on your club, only your club will absorb your mind. If you focus on your ball, only your ball will absorb your mind. Wherever you place your focus, your mind will be absorbed. You don't want absorption — you want flow. Localizing the mind limits the mind. Unless your mind flows freely throughout your body, it will not be available for whatever needs it.

In golf, you don't want just your hands or feet to function properly. You want everything to function properly. Putting your mind in just one place, you fall into what Buddhists call "one-sidedness." So don't ask yourself the self-defeating question of where you should put your mind.

To get the mind to flow freely throughout the body is a matter of discipline. In the martial arts and other disciplines, teachers instruct their pupils in the classic distinction between "right mind" and "confused mind."

Right mind is like water. Confused mind is like ice. Right mind is intuitive, flowing, liquid, useful. In its liquid state, water can be used universally: to quench your thirst, wash your clothes, clean your hands. Confused mind is intellectual, congealed, frozen, impractical. If you stop or "freeze" your mind in your hands or feet, the other parts of your body will not perform. The key is to forget your mind and let it flow so that your entire body becomes one.

When a master deems his pupil a proficient swordsman, he makes a certificate by taking a paint brush, dipping it in ink, and drawing a big circle on a piece of parchment. That's all the certificate contains, a big circle. The circle symbolizes two things. First, it suggests a mirror — the Zen symbol of clarity and inner wisdom. Second, it suggests no mind, or emptiness — the Zen precept of trusting your intuitive self.

Let your mind flow like water throughout your body. Unite technique and intuition. Once you can make your practice swing and your actual swing natural and intuitive, take a piece of paper and draw a circle on it. You've earned your certificate!

WHO AM I?

What are you really doing when you work on your golf game? The parts of your game — putting, chipping, driving — like the parts of yourself, are constantly changing. To study your golf game is to study yourself. Your golf game reflects exactly who you are. Your game is an extension of you. To understand your game is to understand yourself. Golf both molds and expresses your unique character.

All golfers eventually face two serious roadblocks — one early on and one later. The first one is "not knowing." As a beginning golfer you are ignorant about the game. The rules, the techniques, the equipment, the etiquette — everything is new. However, with the requisite determination and interest, you learn quickly.

The second one is "knowing." After you practice and play, golf becomes quite familiar to you. Your muscles develop a habitual sense of the swing. Your body eventually learns more or less what to do. You gain competence. Your satisfaction grows. You play more and more. Now you "know." Not knowing turns into knowing. In the state of knowing, however, you are forced to confront who you are as a golfer and as a person.

Ask the same question of golf that you ask of yourself: "Who am I?" If you can't answer that question about yourself, then look closely at your golf game. The answer is right there. But that answer will come only when you really start to struggle with your game. For example, if your putting is suddenly a shambles and you work hard to regain it, you will begin to learn about yourself. Confront your golf troubles head on, and you will learn about yourself. You will grow.

Those golf troubles contain the potential for real growth. Either you deal with your golf problems or you run from them. It's the choice between opening up and shutting down, between growing and stagnating.

Golf is fickle. That's why the profound lessons of golf are so deeply spiritual. The intimate questions you may ask your psychotherapist or minister are the same troubling questions you ask yourself about golf. Golfers are in constant dialogue with their souls. "Am I the golfer that I think I am?" "Do I really know what I think I know?" "Can I do what I think I can do?"

These questions return you to where you started. Doubt takes you in a circle. At first you try to ignore the questions. But you can't swat them away like gnats. Some day you will have to deal with who you are. Maybe that day will be just before your last heartbeat. Maybe sooner.

You may think it's your lousy putting or your wicked slice that you're working on. What you are really working on is yourself! Your frustrations may actually be your salvation. Respect and honor them. They will lead you to self-knowledge. Golf miseries are gifts in disguise.

These troubles are merely a rest stop on your journey. They allow you to be quiet and deliberate, relaxed and steady, mindful and awake before you move ahead. You won't know whether you or your game is on the right path unless you pause momentarily to see where you are. The point here is that your golf path and spiritual path are connected. In fact, everything in the universe is connected.

Golf is not just some game. Golf is *you*. Golf is your chosen and beloved means of gaining a larger and deeper perspective of who you are. When you transform your golf game — your tempo, rhythm, ball striking — you transform your self.

Golf, with its enigmas and inconsistencies, is your way to contact your unchallenged self. That's one big reason why golf is in your life in the first place. If the disillusion hadn't intrigued you, you would have taken up gardening. When you are totally secure, what incentive is there to look inside yourself? Golf forces you to turn inward. How wonderful! It's dark and dangerous in there. You may not know what you'll find. Turning inward means investigating who you are.

When your game goes sour — and it always will — you'll experience the dark abyss, the vast gap between who you are and who you think you are. You'll be humbled and disillusioned. But you'll also be fortunate. Here's your big chance to find out who you really are. Thank your lucky stars for your golf troubles. It's like the time you got laid off from your old job. It forced you to find a far better one.

Only when the wheels come off will you find your true perspective and inner strength. Only when the wheels come off will you progress. You need them to come off to teach you what's really important in your life.

In Albert Camus's novel *The Stranger*, the main character is a prisoner awaiting execution. Lying on his bed in his cell one day, the condemned murderer gazes up through the skylight. For the first time in his life, he realizes the beautiful blue sky. Until that moment, he never realized the blue sky was such a miracle.

That's when the prisoner vows — during his final three days — to cherish the miracle of being alive.

Golf is never the way you want it to be. Golf is the way it is. You are never the way you want to be. You are the way you are. Discover the joy in ordinary things and experiences. Have the honesty and wisdom to accept yourself for who you are in order to become less judgmental of yourself and others. Simply accept yourself and your game as being entirely okay. The way to nourish your higher self is by spending your life loving what you do.

What you should seek from golf is personal growth. Self-knowledge is the ultimate growth. Everything else can wait! Growth implies new strength, new sincerity, and new awareness. You may think you're simply working on your golf game. What you're really working on is yourself. Golf compels you to find the answer to the question, "Who am I?"

THE NEED TO WIN

Imagine this: you're playing in a weekend tournament. With three holes to go, you're in the lead. Up to this point, you've played well. You've been consistently making putts and hitting fairways and greens. To win you need only grind out these last holes. No big deal! But on the sixteenth hole, you begin to lose focus. Your mind is already on winning: the prize money, the trophy, the congratulations.

You feel your energy and confidence leak. Suddenly, you're not the same golfer. You start to question everything: your skills, club selection, yardage, course strategy. Everything seems different. Even time seems different. Burning with the desire to win, you can't relax. Your new goal is winning, not playing. You've lost the feeling of being harmonious and whole. You're like *two* golfers now — divided between present and future, means and ends.

Thoughts of winning are rampant. It's like you've got a cell phone on your belt and someone keeps calling and calling to tell you that you're going to win. Instead of turning off your cell phone, you keep answering it! You're trying to play golf and talk on the phone at the same time.

Although you fight to gain self-control, your game falls

apart. You finish with two bogeys and a double bogey, and lose by a stroke.

Why you lost is obvious. With the future win on your mind, you couldn't *think* right. With desire in your heart, you couldn't *feel* right. Without right thinking and right feeling, right golf isn't possible. Your mind and heart, filled with need, have no room for composure and awareness. Adrift in the future, you are absent in the present. Your mind is AWOL. When you feel things coming unglued during competition, there are some key things you can do.

First, stay in the moment. Only the present moment belongs to you. The future is an illusion. The past is dead. Between these two eternities is the present. That's where you belong. When you leave the present moment, you invite distraction.

Be like the grass growing on the course. Grass exists moment by moment. It doesn't dream or desire to grow big and tall. When you cool the flames of desire, time becomes meaningless. When you desire nothing, you are like the grass growing naturally all by itself. Create the illusion of timelessness. Become less time-conscious and less time-dependent.

Second, slow down. The impulse to do everything fast will ruin you. Pay attention to your timing. Don't yank your driver from your bag. Remove it slowly. Walk slowly. Scratch your head slowly. Stop equating going fast with getting results. It's just the opposite. Going fast means that you're feeling and reacting to pressure. Going slowly, however, means that you are managing the pressure. Going slowly means refusing to be a victim of pressure.

Speeding up is like an addiction. It literally gives you a "rush." Step outside yourself momentarily and become a detached observer. See yourself speeding up everything, playing like a fast-food junkie. Hungry for burgers and fries, you want to eat as much and as fast as you can. You know that fast food is bad for your health. You know that eating fast is bad for your digestion. So slow down.

Third, empty your boat. Throw some cargo overboard. You can't play well when you're full. Play empty! Empty of what? Empty of dreams, desires, ego, worry, doubt, tension, fear, and confusion. To play well, you must empty yourself of dreams and desires. They create muscular tension, making it that much harder for you to swing freely and naturally.

Emptiness is revered among Eastern thinkers. In the West, emptiness implies something negative, something missing, like a tank without any gas. In the East, emptiness implies something positive. Emptiness is synonymous with freedom. The freedom to be who you really are!

According to Taoists, the perfect human being is an empty boat. Being empty means being unconstrained. That's what you need when you are playing: freedom. Freedom of movement, of tension, of desire, of failure. This point was discussed by Chuang-Tzu. He wrote:

> When an archer is shooting for fun, he has all his skill. If he shoots for a brass buckle, he is already nervous. If he shoots for a prize of gold, he goes blind — or sees two targets — he is out of his mind. His skill has not changed, but the prize divides him. He cares. He thinks more of winning than of shooting — and the need to win drains him of his power.

The archer's craving to win divides his focus and drains his energy. When Chuang-Tzu's archer competes for gold, he can't shoot freely and naturally. So too with you. When you become empty, you are free. When you become full, you are constrained. Empty your desires and dreams. Throw everything overboard and lighten up.

Fourth, focus on your breathing. By focusing on your breathing, you will unclutter your mind and relax yourself. Lose yourself in your breathing. Don't focus on anything but breathing. Make breathing — not winning — your main goal. Make yourself into a self-conscious breathing machine.

Chuang-Tzu said, "True men breathe through their heels." He meant you should breathe deeply through your belly and hold it for a moment. Then breathe out calmly, slowly, and totally. After a slight break, breathe in again. Breathe in and out slowly and steadily. Every time you breathe out, feel yourself becoming more relaxed and composed.

Establish a rhythm and a cadence to your breathing. If you need to hum, like Fuzzy Zoeller or Fred Funk, then hum as you focus on your breath. Remain mindful of your breathing. When you lose track of your breathing, return to it. Lose yourself in the breathing. With slow and rhythmic breathing, your muscles will relax. Before you hit a shot, exhale deeply, then swing. Relaxation and mindful breathing go hand in hand. Breath control will greatly help.

Fifth, adjust your ego. Since the need to win flows from your ego, you need to control it. Your ego desperately wants people to know you're "somebody." The perceived opinions of others make up your ego. Ask yourself: "Self, how important is it that people know I am a somebody — a winner?"

Playing from your ego puts pressure on you. Everything gets heavy. Your ego is your imagined self. It's not the real you! The real you is different. The real you doesn't care what others think. The real you doesn't need to win to prove you're somebody. The real you already knows you're somebody. Become egoless. Give yourself a reality check from time to time. Ask yourself honestly whether your real self or your ego is running the show.

Finally, have fun. Having fun and playing competitively are

not mutually exclusive. Having fun will relax you, providing the calmness and freedom to play well. Having fun is the way to get results. It means checking your seriousness at the door and being loose enough to perform at your best. When you scan your body and feel uptight, lighten up and remind yourself to have fun. Instead of finding things wrong, enjoy what's right. Have fun *and* play competitively. Then there's no conflict.

The perfect archer, even during competition, has fun! You "play" golf — you don't "produce" golf. Golf is process, not product. When you have fun, when you savor life's sweetest gifts, you can barely hold the joy. Whether you play golf or play a flute — for heaven's sake — have fun and play from your heart. The only way to create beautiful music is by playing from your heart.

Life offers you billions of momentary chances to win. Each passing moment gives you only one chance. So fill each moment with joy. Live each moment with love and respect. Then one chance will be enough. Then you always win!

THE TEE CEREMONY

Drinking tea and playing golf are closely related ceremonial events, both of which started as routine activities. In Japan the tea ceremony goes back centuries. Japanese philosophers and artists would sip tea, exchange stories, read poetry, arrange flowers, and enjoy nature.

Then Japanese tea drinkers gradually made up formal rules, used special utensils, and observed certain practices. Tea drinking was no longer just tea drinking. It became an occasion to practice one's tranquillity, reverence, harmony, and humility.

As a golfer, imagine yourself at a tea ceremony. It begins with three or four close friends who share your love of tea. At a cottage nestled in a grove of pines near a trickling mountain brook, you and your friends retreat to nature.

Outside the cottage is a rustic wooden bench where everyone sits waiting for the signal to begin the ceremony. From the bench, you see a path leading into the tea master's manicured garden adorned with flowers and shrubs. You enjoy talking quietly with your friends. A bell chimes to signal that it's time for the ceremony to begin. You remove your sandals and enter the ten-foot-square tea room under the thatched roof.

You hear the sounds of the kettle boiling the water. You smell the pine trees outside and the faint trace of jasmine incense burning inside. Everything is quiet except for the breeze outside, rustling the trees. The mountain brook, providing the pure water for the tea, gurgles faintly in the background. You revel in the warm hospitality of the tea room.

You forget about your worldly concerns. No beepers. No cell phones. You aim only to immerse yourself in the ceremonial drinking of tea with close friends. Nothing else matters. You feel warm and comfortable. You are in harmony with everything around you. A mysterious reverence fills you.

Your host brings in a plate of rice cakes, tea cups, a bamboo whisk, a large bowl, a porcelain tea caddy, and some green tea. You study the worn utensils, each having its own peculiar charm. You and your friends are served one by one. You gently hold your tea cup. Watchful and considerate, you wait for everyone to be served. You are ever mindful of others. Each, in turn, sips some tea. Among the four of you there is an uncommon civility. After several hours of sipping tea and quiet conversation, the ceremony ends. You say farewell, bow, and leave.

The tea ceremony, like golf, has rules for etiquette, the setting, and the use of utensils. Today, Japanese frequently use the term *mucha*, meaning "It's not tea!" It means that something is outside the rules. It's like saying, "That's not golf," when your partner gives himself a six-foot putt.

There are two key rules in "the way of tea." The first is to be your own teacher. Learn through close observation. The second is to show first your *love*, then your *dexterity*, and finally your *perseverance* in the art of tea. Both of these rules are axiomatic in golf.

The rules are not only about making, serving, and drinking tea. They are about developing your self-awareness. According to tea masters, tea drinkers must practice four basic principles: harmony, reverence, purity, and tranquillity.

Harmony means maintaining perfect balance with yourself, others, and nature — everything in moderation. Reverence means recognizing your spiritual relationship with all things, living and nonliving — connecting with something larger than yourself. Purity means feeling both orderly and cleansed — mental and physical freshness. Finally, tranquillity means being in a state of complete relaxation — a state of dynamic stillness. These principles are spiritual medicine for tea drinkers and golfers.

The Japanese tea ceremony is all about nourishing one's awareness. "If you pour a cup of tea," Chögyam Trungpa (a famous Tibetan master) wrote, "you are aware of extending your arm and touching your hand to the teapot, lifting it and pouring the water. Finally, the water touches your teacup and fills it, and you stop pouring and put the teapot down precisely.... You become aware that each precise movement has dignity. We have long forgotten that activities can be simple and precise. Every act of our lives can contain simplicity and precision and thus can have tremendous beauty and dignity."

Golf the *activity* is circumscribed by normal time and space. Golf the *ceremony* transcends normal time and space. In the activity of golf, a morning dew drop on the fairway is just a morning dew drop. In the ceremony of golf, a morning dew drop on the fairway is a prism reflecting the whole universe. Walk your own fairway, leaving your tracks in the dew. The faint bell that you hear is the signal that the tee ceremony has begun.

THE MIRROR

If you're like most golfers, you have a distorted view of yourself. And that's precisely why you stagnate. What you think or feel about yourself doesn't matter — it's irrelevant. What matters is what you actually are. What's relevant is what's in the mirror.

In the East, a mirror is a profound symbol of self-awareness. A mirror reflects things not as you perceive them but as they are. Eastern masters often tell their pupils "to polish" or "to dust off" their mirrors. Essentially, these masters are advising their students to wake up, to look deeply, and to see things as they are.

Consider how teaching pros — who act as self-awareness coaches — use videotape. First, they videotape you from several different angles. You need to see what your swing actually looks like from the front, back, and side — and (if possible) from overhead.

Second, they review the videotape with you. If they see something wrong in your setup, they will stop the frame and make you aware of it. They will pointedly ask you, "Do you see how much you're swaying here?" or "Do you see how upright you're standing at address?" They are engaging your self-awareness powers.

Third, they compare your swing with a model swing. If your posture is a problem, they will show you a videotape of Nick Faldo or Tom Kite so you can model their posture. Viewing videotape gives you an objective view of yourself.

Fourth, teaching pros will have you set up and swing in front of a mirror. They want you to see yourself modeling correctly. They want you to look carefully and critically at yourself — to bring self-awareness to your looking.

Fifth, they take you back to the practice area and have you hit shots. They want to teach you how to integrate self-awareness into your doing.

Your self-awareness is like a radar detection system. If your radar system isn't being used, you'll never detect what's going on around you. Often your problems will appear on somebody else's radar screen before they appear on yours. It's so hard to see yourself. That's why you need to look in the mirror, use videotape, or rely on the radar systems of others.

To get a fix on your game, start with a mirror, a golf book, and a keen sense of self-awareness. Look at your setup in a mirror. (A poor setup, according to many golf instructors, is the root of most people's problems.) Look critically at your grip, ball position, alignment, stance, posture. Pay special attention to your posture. Use illustrations or photos in golf books and magazines as models. Make comparisons and take notes.

Practice swing drills in the mirror. Do exactly what the drill suggests. In a posture drill, for example, bend at the knees, stick out your butt, let your hands hang down, point your belt buckle at the ball, place your feet shoulder-width apart. Do exactly what the pro is doing. Don't adopt a posture that you feel or think is right. Adopt a posture that in your mirror matches up with the pro's posture. Let the mirror decide.

Now use the mirror to see your swing in slow motion. Pay

close attention to the position of the club and body throughout the swing — during the takeaway, backswing, position at the top, downswing, release, follow-though. Put (or have someone put) some tape on the mirror to mark the positions of your chin and spine when you address the ball. Then swing your club in slow motion.

Check whether your chin stays in back of the ball throughout the swing. Also check whether your spine angle (the angle formed at address between legs and spine) remains the same throughout the swing. Maintaining your spine angle is critical. If that angle changes, it means you're moving too much during the swing. Pay close attention to the plane of the left arm.

A mirror, like an X-ray, is a diagnostic tool. You may require an orthopedist to detect a subtle hairline fracture on an X-ray. But you don't require an orthopedist to detect a severely broken bone. You can see that for yourself. Similarly, you don't need a golf pro to detect a fundamental crack in your setup or swing. You can do that for yourself.

Consider what happened to Harry Potter. Before Harry saw his reflection in the Mirror of Erised at the Hogwarts School, he was like a lowly worm. Living with the Dursleys, who never gave a damn about him, Harry was frustrated and stagnant. But after he viewed himself in the magic mirror, Harry suddenly changed. He realized his precise goals, found his rightful path, and developed his true character.

Look deeply into your magic mirror. When you reflect honestly and critically on what you see, you'll be transformed, too. You won't be a lowly golf worm anymore.

DISCONNECTION

Golf can make you feel very large. When you feel large, everything is connected — your body, mind, swing, club, world. If you don't play golf for a living, you probably play to express your deepest passions. But when your game goes sour, you'll lose heart. Without heart, nothing will sustain you.

When you become disconnected, everything seems fragmented. Your mind separates from your body, breath from mind, club from hand, hands from legs, shoulders from arms, hands from mind. To reconnect, start linking with everything around you. Don't view the trees, the grass, the ball, the club, other players, other swings, other tempers as totally apart from you. Connect with everything, especially yourself. Be like the sky that spans everything.

Charlie "Yardbird" Parker, the great jazz musician, viewed his saxophone as an extension of his body. Both musician and golfer begin by learning the basics. They practice the basics over and over until they master them. Gradually, the music merges with the musician and the golf merges with the golfer. When this merging happens, the joy of playing the saxophone or playing golf will overflow inside you.

When you connect with music or golf, you'll play at a new level. By playing, you're connecting with a higher power. A different feeling arises. Before, the saxophone or golf club was separate from you. Now it's a part of you. Suddenly, the saxophone or golf club feels so much more powerful.

Carl Jung claimed that one-third of his patients suffered from no clinically defined neurosis. They simply felt a pervasive emptiness — a vague disconnection — in their lives. If that's the way you feel, then you may need to become more inclusive, open, and expansive. Don't view golf with just your head. View it also with your heart. Wholeness requires that you open your heart. Your heart is not just a muscle in your chest. It's your center for golf energy and wisdom.

Let's say you make perfect contact with your 6-iron. You feel elated. Your feelings will tell you when you make perfect contact and when you're in perfect balance. Your feelings (not your thoughts) will tell you when your swing is sufficiently rhythmic and harmonious. Golf instructors don't tell their students to "think the clubhead." They tell their students to "feel the clubhead."

Disconnection is a feeling, not a thought. If you feel disconnected, perhaps you're thinking too much. Thinking accesses golf knowledge. Feeling, however, accesses golf wisdom. To reconnect with golf's hidden wholeness, balance feeling and thinking, wisdom and knowledge.

When you disconnect the plug of your illuminated desk lamp from the wall socket, the light will go out. So too with golf. When you disconnect feelings from thoughts in your swing, your "golf light" will go out. But you don't have to be an electrical engineer to know that the lights are off. Right?

THE MANTRA

In the East, mantras are used to focus, stabilize, and free the mind. Mantras are ideal for uptight golfers. A mantra will make you more awake, more refreshed, more centered. For thousands of years, people of all cultures have used them. Mantras are repetitive and sacred sounds or chants to invoke inspiration and power. It sounds kooky, but, using mantras, I have had some great rounds!

Mantras use sound energy to bring joy, stillness, and clarity into the mind. The word *mantra* means "that which protects the mind." When you're anxious and upset on the golf course, your golf mantra can protect your mind by dissolving tension and negativity.

Mantras are based on the principle that all action is accompanied by sound. Sound is a form of vibrational energy. But a mantra is a special sound, a special form of energy. It expresses condensed spiritual truths. It is the ultimate sound. Each syllable is packed with spiritual power. Vibrating with incredible power, mantras are viewed as blessings, inspirations, and protections from beyond.

Mantras work by taking the sound energy of the chant and

moving it through your mind and body. They keep mind and body in balance. Their power comes from the breath. Chanting silently or aloud, you unite breath, awareness, and mantra as one. The mantra "protects the mind" from becoming too random, too scattered, too negative.

Repeating the mantra over and over, you create an inner resonance. It's like having a generator or dynamo purring inside you. This vibrational energy will induce an amazing sense of inner calmness and renewal. When you start to tense up on the course, recite your golf mantra to create instant harmony and balance.

Monks chant their mantras several million times throughout their lives. Repetitious chanting builds up a tremendous reservoir of spiritual energy. The power of the mantra lies in its repetition. Some mantras, passed down for generations, have been chanted for thousands of years. Reciting a mantra, like following your breath or focusing on an object, "brings the mind home," as Tibetans say.

In times of stress, repeat your mantra over and over to gain clarity and focus as you stand or walk. Begin by breathing slowly. Invent your own mantra. That's the way all mantras are born. Select words that have an impact on your soul. Any sound that feels beautiful and joyful in your heart will do. The sounds do not have to belong to any language. Choose a relaxing sound that resonates deep inside.

Your mantra will be more penetrating and powerful if your lips and tongue are still. Chant rhythmically and "loudly within" at your own pace. Feel the vibration of energy circulate from your head to your feet. A mantra's effect is that of a stone tossed into a quiet pond. Ripples of energy will emanate from a center point.

The instant you stop chanting you will enjoy a poignant moment of awareness. Savor it! Soon, however, your mind will fill again with distracting thoughts. Chanting will restore inner calmness and focus. Reciting your mantra is like putting your golf game on automatic pilot. It focuses you and brings you back on track. As you chant, return to your breathing. Become your quiet self.

Whatever happens during chanting, let it be. Don't interfere with it or manipulate it. Reciting your mantra will soon become totally natural. Go with it, and you will experience precious glimpses of serenity and joy.

Mind protection through sound vibration is an ancient practice. Native American youngsters sent on a vision quest are taught to be receptive and alert for a sacred chant. After days of fasting and ritualized ordeal, the youngsters finally hear the sacred chant — a sign that the Great Spirit has blessed and protected them. From that moment on, they recite their sacred chant from the Great Spirit. They never forget it.

On my own vision quest, the "Great Golf Spirit" sent me two sacred chants: "Green grass, white ball, blue sky" and "I'm one with my body." When you play golf, listen carefully. Perhaps the Great Golf Spirit will bless you with a sacred chant. It will stay with you until your last fairway, your last round, your last heartbeat.

EMPTY YOUR GOLF BAG

Cleansing and purifying the mind is a very religious notion. Christians use the term *ablution* to denote the washing away of sin by water. Buddhists rely on meditation practices to purify the so-called impurities of the mind.

In Western cultures, learning means loading up the mind. Learning for members of Western culture is like getting dressed. You put on your underwear, socks, shirt, pants, shoes, hat. Then you say to yourself, "Great, now I'm fully dressed." In the West, to learn is to program the mind.

In Eastern cultures, however, learning means unloading the mind. Learning for members of Eastern culture is more like getting undressed. You remove your hat, shoes, pants, shirt, socks, underwear. Then you say to yourself, "Ahh, now I'm naked." In the East, to learn is to deprogram the mind.

The simple truth is that learning involves both loading and unloading, adding and subtracting, programming and deprogramming, getting dressed and getting undressed. Practice both modes of learning according to your needs. Ask yourself the following questions: How much of your accumulated golf knowledge do you actually need? How much of it actually helps? Are these layers of accumulated knowledge impeding your growth? Is it time to give your golf mind a hot shower and a thorough scrubbing to remove those layers? Is it time to return to your "beginner's mind"?

YOUR MENTOR

You'll know immediately if you've met your golf mentor. Like any great teacher, your golf mentor will awaken something dormant in you. When you find your mentor, you'll start to grow.

In one Islamic tradition, the moment your true teacher looks at you for the first time, you are born again. This is what Sufis call "The Glance." This is an important moment. It's your second birth. That's when you'll know you've got the right teacher.

You must be able to see yourself in your mentor. If that's not possible, you have the wrong mentor. Mentors have learned to manifest their talents. With your mentor's help, you will some-day manifest yours.

An *ordinary* teacher provides you with the basic elements of golf — the mechanics. A *good* teacher provides you with golf's physical and mental elements. This teacher knows how to merge these elements. A *mentor*, however, provides you with the physical, mental, and spiritual elements of golf. A mentor imparts both wisdom and knowledge.

A mentor will teach you to become golf — to live golf. This means that there is never an instant when your mentor is not teaching. Even when your mentor eats, sleeps, walks, talks, or chops wood, he or she is still teaching you golf. In fact, some of the more subtle learning takes place off the course or out of the practice area. Watch the way your mentor drives a car, eats a sandwich, or signs a check. Each of those moments is a golf lesson! From your mentor, you get a sublime feeling that transcends knowledge. You'll learn golf wisdom.

A mentor has two roles: to arouse the creative power of golf inside you and to support you while you tap your inner power. Through a mentor, you'll experience a union of various energies. You will unite with all those spirits who influenced your mentor — in my case, with Jones, Hogan, Snead, and Nicklaus. Ultimately, you will unite with golf.

Don't go to your mentor simply for answers. Anyone who's dogmatic and has all the answers doesn't understand golf. Answers will satisfy only half your appetite. You want to live the questions. You want to learn how golf changes you from the inside out. Mentors will give you new ways to look at your golf problems. A mentor will fill your heart, not your head.

Don't assume that your mentor will suddenly make golf easy and simple. Golf will always remain a mystery and a struggle. However, your mentor will make the arduous wonderful. You'll learn from your mentor to remain open. The greatest gift a mentor can instill in you is a commitment to keep growing. To grow means to remain open, to let the creative energy of golf flow through you. By remaining open you'll withstand the difficulties and pressures of golf.

Unlike the ordinary teacher, who directs the energy of learning to himself or herself, the mentor directs the energy of learning to the student. Your mentor is like a well. You drink the water from the well. The well's energy becomes your energy.

A mentor appears only when the student is ready. Consider your qualities as a student. Perhaps your approach to learning is blocking your growth. The quality of your mentor is important. But what's more important is your willingness to grow. You can blame the teacher or the teaching. Or you can blame yourself!

Look around for a mentor. But choose only one. Your mentor is a doorway to golf. You can go through only one doorway at a time. Settle on the mentor who will expand your awareness. Select a wise mentor whose style and energy resonates in you. Above all, select a mentor who will never limit you. Then get to work.

A wise mentor will tell you to keep a log. The log will record your development. Lessons will get repeated. But always with a slightly different nuance. Your log will be a reminder of what to hold on to and what to let go of.

Finding a golf mentor is like finding a spiritual guide. After Simon and Andrew, who were simple fishermen, found Jesus, they remained fishermen, but they became totally new fishermen. After you find your golf mentor, you'll still be a golfer — but you'll be a totally new golfer.

GOLF ROBOT

All golfers have some bad habits — like hitting from the top, swinging too fast, moving off the ball, or regripping the club. When you can't seem to shake these habits, what should you do?

First, understand that you've been playing golf this way for years. These habits have taken root. Don't expect them to just go away. Your mind isn't capable of that kind of power. Your body isn't capable of that kind of control. You're a slave to a fast swing, or a tight grip, or a strong right hand. These things now happen automatically. You're programmed to swing this way. You've become a golf robot!

To avoid making the same robotic mistakes, you need to reprogram yourself by becoming more mindful. It's not particularly hard to be mindful. The problem is *remembering* to be mindful. To reprogram your robotic swing, you need to think about thinking. You need to remember to remember.

Second, start viewing a round of golf as a test of alertness and perceptual intelligence. Think of golf both as an action and as a state of being. Notice every action, perception, feeling. If a monk can make a meditation out of washing dishes, chopping wood, or drinking tea, certainly you can make a meditation out of playing golf. Don't distinguish between "golf as meditation" and "meditation as golf." Consider them the same!

Recently, I lunched with a friend who discussed his latest research project. From his lunch bag he removed some cherries. Without even looking at them, he started to remove the stems and pop the fruit into his mouth. Before he finished chewing and swallowing the previous cherry, he put another in his mouth. He wasn't the least bit aware of what he was doing. He ate the cherries like a robot.

If a robot ate cherries, it would eat them without really tasting, smelling, or seeing them. When you eat cherries mechanically, you never eat them at all. If you play golf like a robot, you don't play at all.

Program yourself to be mindful of every single action. When you take your 5-iron from your bag, do it mindfully. Remove it slowly. Observe its shiny surface. Hear it clink against the other irons. Feel the cold blade in your hand. Appreciate the club's beautiful design and craftsmanship.

Then gently hold the club. Become conscious of every movement of your fingers, hands, and arms. Feel the spongy Winn grip in your palm. Savor every small gesture you make with the club. In fact, divide choosing and using a club into as many separate, small acts as possible.

Next, take a practice swing. Take a deep breath. Fill your lungs with calmness and relaxation. Attach yourself to the present moment. Caress the club. Feel your hands release the clubhead. Feel the tension ooze from you. Sense the folly of swinging the club too quickly and gripping it too tightly.

Understand, confront, and consider your bad golf habits as silly impediments to your game. They're silly not because some golf guru said so but because they feel silly. Don't intellectualize about them. Just intuit from your whole being what feels right.

To deprogram yourself is to witness yourself. Watch what you do. Don't pay attention only to your swing, your grip, your stance, your posture. When you walk, walk slowly and mindfully. When you swing, swing slowly and mindfully. When you breathe, breathe slowly and mindfully. Magnify the most obvious detail. Pay attention to the totality of golf.

WALKING MEDITATION

Walking properly is not as simple as it appears. It takes practice. Most golfers do not know how to walk. Compare the way you walk with the way most pros walk. Tour pros "walk in beauty," as the Navajos say. The pros are in no hurry. They stroll down the fairway. They amble casually around the green. They walk as if they weren't trying to get anywhere.

When your mind is in a rush, your whole body speeds up. As you go from tee to green to tee again, your thoughts dictate how your body should move. You're not even aware that your mind is signaling your body to rush.

Golfers have what Buddhists call "monkey mind." A cluttered and distracted mind, like a monkey, swings randomly and tirelessly from branch to branch. It chatters nonstop. It won't stay silent and still. Your mind will never be completely quiet. But the sheer act of walking — expending physical energy — helps focus your mind. Like any form of exercise, walking releases tension. That's why many healthy golfers prefer to walk rather than ride in a cart. It makes sense.

Don't expect to quiet your mind automatically. Walking mindfully doesn't require a lot of concentration. But you need to pay close attention to every step. If you take walking for granted, you overlook what a miracle it really is. It requires incredible coordination, balance, and control. Just ask rehab patients and PTs about the miracle of walking. When you walk the course, don't take the miracle of walking for granted. Walking mindfully is your lifeline to the joys of golf.

Consider the pleasure of walking on a beautiful golf course. As afternoon vanishes, you walk at sundown. Walk slowly and enjoy it. Don't walk just to get to your ball! The purpose of a walking meditation is to be fully present in each step, in each breath. Slow down. Coordinate your breathing and walking. Let your breathing — not your mind — dictate your pace. For each inhale, take two or three steps, whatever your lungs allow. For each exhale, take two or three steps. Follow your breathing. It's the key to all meditation.

Feel your golf shoes touch the warm earth. Walk in the spirit of caressing the ground. Let the energy of walking radiate through your feet, legs, knees, hips, pelvis, and upper body. Don't look around. Keep your gaze at a forty-five-degree angle or directly ahead of you. Don't look down at your feet. Just *be* with every step. Remain focused. Make walking an act of dynamic stillness. Accept each step, each breath, each moment.

Walking mindfully will bring you back to your center. Walking is like prayer or fasting or chanting or any spiritual discipline. Among Buddhists, archery is considered a spiritual discipline. Aiming the arrow at the target, the Zen archer essentially aims the arrow at *himself*. Obviously, the archer learns about archery. But he is really learning about himself. Your walking is like an arrow that will lead you closer to yourself. Mindful walking returns you to your calm center. That's your real target.

When you begin a walking meditation, you'll hear an impatient inner voice telling you to rush. Your inner voice is such a natural part of you that you won't even notice it. But that's your ego talking. Don't let it ruin your walking meditation. Your ego, if you let it, will create expectations. For example, if you expect to see your ball sitting up in a perfect lie, your whole walk focuses only on your ball. Expectations create tension, block energy, and set up disappointment. So walk mindfully. No ego means no expectations! Just focus on your breathing.

Allow walking to pry open your imagination and your consciousness. It's a powerful tool to tap your inner self, your deeper knowledge, your higher power. Saint Augustine wrote, "Solvitur ambulando," "It is solved by walking." Walking mindfully, you'll hear a whisper deep within you. This is the whisper that can solve your golf problems. This is the whisper that walking meditation honors.

When a tenth-century monk asked Ummon, his master, "What is the meaning of the Tao?" Ummon simply said, "Walk on!" So walk on, Dear Golfer!

THE SILVER BELT BUCKLE

Just below your navel, at the silver belt buckle, is your center. The Japanese call it *hara*; the Chinese call it *tan t'ien*; yogis call it the *third chakra*. The English language, however, doesn't have an adequate word for the body's center. But that doesn't matter. Just know that it exists.

Take a deep abdominal breath, and you will feel your center expand. Your center is both a physical place and a spiritual place. When you become aware of its presence, you'll feel more grounded, balanced, and relaxed.

You probably consider your head as your golfing center. If your head is your center, then that's where your golf game originates. But if you center your golf consciousness in your head, your body will lag behind. And you don't want that. You want to unite mind and body.

Today, researchers tell us that consciousness permeates your entire body. Messenger molecules interconnect and communicate with the trillions of cells in your body. Consciousness is not a physical place but a relationship. Quite simply, consider shifting your golf center to your navel. It's a great place for it.

The grace and agility of all great athletes originate at their center. When you watch great athletes in action, don't watch their heads — watch their center. The same is true of great golfers. They move from their center. Watch their silver belt buckles. The center is the key to posture, stance, swing, tempo, and balance. The big muscles, attached to the pelvis, lie at the center. These are the primary golf muscles. The small muscles, attached to the periphery, are the secondary golf muscles.

Golf is both doing and being, both dynamic activity and serene awareness. The big problem for golfers is the inability to understand and integrate doing and being. However, when you play from your center, you merge these two energies.

Energy doesn't mean muscular force. It means a flow of natural and rhythmic power. When you swing with raw muscle, you lose your connection with your center. Doing and being separate. To use "energy" means connecting with your center. Being "energized" means being calm and alert, receptive and flowing.

The Chinese call this life-flowing energy *chi*. Don't try to define or understand chi. Just try to feel it. Consider chi the energy flowing outward from your center, then back again.

The Japanese center, *hara*, is the point of bliss. When your energy passes through the *hara* in sports or sex or combat, you experience bliss. All "peak experiences" — to use Abraham Maslow's term — pass through your center, your *hara*. To be pumped up is to be in touch with your hara.

With consciousness at the *hara*, the body doesn't think — it just responds. At the *hara* level, the act comes first. Thought comes second. For example, you don't solve a math problem at the *hara* level. It's not like that. At the *hara* level, you'll hit a crisp 7-iron over a pond or drive your ball straight down a tight fairway.

To place your consciousness at the *hara* is to play from your center. In the performing arts, martial arts, and sports, you learn to reverse consciousness. You act first. You think later. You do this only by discovering, understanding, and trusting your center.

Playing from your center means that you become more awake, more whole, more "actual." (Maslow used the term *self-actualization.*) It means that at birth you are not actual, just potential. Fulfilling your potential and becoming "actual" is entirely up to you. Nature doesn't actualize you. You actualize yourself. Lao-Tzu wrote, "Abide at the center of your being; for the more you leave it, the less you learn."

Poor golfers fight the course. Centered golfers merge with the course. If you attack the course, you attack yourself. So let the energy of the course flow *through* you, not *against* you. Absorb the energy of golf. It's the same in the martial arts. You learn to flow *with* your opponent's energy. Poor golfers slash, hack, and flail. Centered golfers flow, dance, and glide.

Every powerful cyclone needs a calm center, or it can't exist. You're the same when you get angry or tense. Anger and tension exist on the periphery. When you return to your center, anger and tension dissipate. You'll get disturbed when you move away from the quiet point at your center. The further you move from your center, the more disturbed you'll get. You can't shake your disturbances. Only if you move closer to your silver belt buckle can you quiet them.

To destroy your energy center is to commit hara-kiri. Don't be concerned about destroying your energy center. Be concerned about never finding it. So start looking for it. It's right under your silver belt buckle.

EGO

The most common "disease" among golfers is not a duck hook, an unruly slice, or an attack of the shanks. It's a disease of the ego called obsession — an excessive attachment to some fixed idea. It doesn't matter if the idea is worthy or unworthy. It's any idea fixed in your mind. The ego fixes it there. Golfers obsess over many things: winning, competing, scoring, playing, rushing, improving, practicing, thinking, experimenting, owning, talking, cheating, judging, complaining, and who knows what else. Golfers even obsess over obsessing!

In Japan, students of archery, judo, aikido, calligraphy, flower arrangement, gardening, and other art forms learn specific techniques. They assiduously practice these Zen arts not just to learn techniques but to learn about themselves. These art forms are paths to spiritual truth and personal growth. By learning spiritual truths, you learn to free yourself from your ego.

However, if your ego rules you, you'll lose your way. Yagyu Tajima, a seventeenth-century Zen swordsman, discussed this key point. In a secret document written to his sons, Yagyu noted the spiritual and psychological elements of all great swordsmen. These elements relate directly to golfers.

First, Yagyu explains that swordsmanship is a way to seek the truth. Like swordsmanship, golf is a spiritual quest for truth. To understand golf is to understand the self. To understand the self is to attain truth.

Second, Yagyu states that swordsmanship demands first your spirit, then your intellect. Today, his words still ring true. To wield a sword smoothly, the mind must also flow smoothly. Sword and golf club must become one with hand and mind.

Third, Yagyu warns about the ego, which prevents you from seeing the truth about yourself. The ego creates "diseases" that cripple the free flow of mind and body. Rooted in the ego, these diseases separate mind from body, spiritual from physical. (Yagyu refers to the obsessive desire for victory as one such disease of the ego!) The sword is the symbolic means of cutting through the ego.

Your desire for victory is an expression of pride. As a part of life, golf is both triumph and defeat. To divide golf into winning and losing, you miss the totality of golf. You miss participating in the triumph and joy of others. Jack Nicklaus is admired widely because he knew how to win and lose graciously.

Your ego will tell you to worship your score, your swing, your clubs, your low handicap, whatever. If you do, you practice an ancient idolatry in which you expect something on the outside to make you happy on the inside.

Your ego may also prompt you to cheat. By knowing and obeying the rules of golf, you honor the game and yourself. There is only one ultimate golf referee, umpire, official, or judge — your conscience. Let it shine! Don't let your ego compromise your integrity. Pay yourself some respect.

Your ego may also prompt you to lavish displays of arrogance. Bobby Jones, unselfish and humble, is honored as both a great golfer and a great sportsman. Gene Sarazen, who competed often against Jones, admired Jones for his ability to consider his opponent first.

Between 1927 and 1935, Jones won an amazing 62 percent of all the British and U.S. championships he entered. By the time he retired at age twenty-eight, he had won thirteen titles, including the Grand Slam. That's remarkable. What's even more remarkable, however, was Jones's ability to leave his opponents with the sincere impression that they played just as well as he did. The only difference, according to Jones, was that he was a bit luckier. How does your ego match up against Jones's?

Unless you see your golf ego for what it is, you will never find golf's ultimate truths. If you don't find golf's ultimate truths, you won't grow. You will always be grasping and clinging. Whether you know it or not, whether you like it or not, golf's real truths never pass through the ego. Golf's real truths pass through the heart. Your heart — not your mind — ultimately determines how much you will grow.

Your ego is a filter that will dim golf's radiance. Your heart is a lens that will magnify golf's radiance.

GRIP PRESSURE

Golf teachers all stress the importance of constant grip pressure. You're taught to maintain a firm grip — not too loose or too tight. You're taught to keep the pressure relatively even between right hand and left hand. (Byron Nelson, among others, taught his pupils to grip the club more tightly in the left hand.) You're taught to relax your grip to release the clubhead.

But you also need to know how to release your mind. What's ultimately gripping the club so tightly is your mind! That's the source of your problem.

What you're gripping so tightly is not only the club but also your desire to win, to excel, to impress. The specific desire really doesn't matter. What matters is that you realize what's behind your tight grip. Energy, according to yogis, is stored in the head and released in the hands. So any tension in your mind will move to your hands!

As you grip the club, sense the mystical connection taking place. Make the act of gripping the club a sacred union, a ceremonial gesture. Grip the club as pros do. In the ritual of the grip, you join mind and body, spirit and object, animate and inanimate. Consider any pressure in your hands a disruption of oneness.

Identify any clinging. Understand what you are clinging to. Then let go. When your energy flows freely — merging body, mind, and spirit — you will sense it.

Never let go merely for the sake of letting go. For example, when you grip your driver, don't release hand pressure without also releasing ego pressure. Release both hands and mind. Simultaneously, release physical and mental stress.

If you understand this connection between hands and the ego, you'll swing smoothly and release the clubhead. Letting go should become a pure act. Letting go simply means becoming empty. Don't invest the act of letting go with any undue pressure or stress.

A famous story illustrates this point.

A student asked his Zen master, "I've got nothing in my mind right now. What should I do next?"

The master replied, "Pick it up." The master was advising his student not just to let go but to let go naturally.

In other words, once you think about not thinking, you're doomed, right? It's like emptying a glass of water. You don't have to think about pouring out the contents. You simply empty it. Do the same on the course when desires jam up your mind.

When you let go, you simply release yourself from illusions. It's like turning off a mental movie projector. Your golf ego projects its cravings onto a big mind-screen. If you allow those cravings to keep rolling inside you, then your ego plays golf while your relaxed self watches.

When you see wear marks on your Winn grips, that's the surest sign that it's time to let go. Your hands and ego — clenched with need and calloused from grasping too tightly — made those wear marks. Just let go.

EITHER-OR GOLF

Absolutes rule golf. Your shot is right or left. You're in bounds or out of bounds. Your ball is on the green or off. You hit the right club or the wrong club. You win or you lose. Your score is true or false. You make or miss the putt. Much of golf is absolute — black and white. This is "either-or" golf.

If you play either-or golf, you probably live your life the same way. You divide your world into good and bad, like and dislike, true and false. However, there's another way to live.

Look at a golf ball. Is it concave or convex? Actually, it's both. The inside cover is concave. The outside cover is convex. The ball's cover does two things: it both separates and unites concave and convex. You can't have a golf ball unless you unite both. They are not just opposites but inseparable entities. The ball's cover is essentially a line. All lines simultaneously separate and unite.

Lines can be both physical and mental. For example, physical lines define a hazard on the course. Mental lines define whether you played well or poorly. Lines are arbitrary. A line becomes a "barrier" when you use it to separate opposites. However, a line is just a line when its use is twofold: to separate *and* unite opposites. The trick in golf is to draw lines without creating barriers.

Barriers disrupt the inherent unity in all things. The ultimate reality of golf lies in recognizing and appreciating the unity of opposites. Golf becomes total frustration when you view everything as either-or. So you miss an easy three-foot putt for par. But then you drain a fifty-footer for birdie. That fifty-footer assumes a lot more meaning. And suddenly golf becomes magical. The contrast between the putt you missed and the one you made is a glimpse of golf wholeness. Joining opposites provides golf with its richness and totality. Don't view the missed and made putts as separate realities. View them as complementary aspects of one unified experience.

Either-or logic invariably breaks down in golf. To denote the fallacy of such logic, the Japanese use the term *mu*. It means "no" or "not." It signifies not this and not that — but both. In fact, the *mu* notion lies at the heart of Zen. To grasp *mu* is to understand unity.

Golf requires a *mu* response. *Mu* neither confirms nor denies. It simply opens and enlarges the issue at hand. Golf isn't this or that — it's always both. If you accentuate only the positive and dismiss the negative, you miss the point of golf. Good shots differ from bad ones as day differs from night. However, without night, day doesn't exist. Ignoring the negative, you remove any possibility of enjoying the positive.

Golf is a sweet melody of opposites. Hold your golf ball in your hand as a reminder of golf's oneness. The ball's cover is not a barrier that separates outer from inner. It's a line that joins both. Play golf by joining opposites. Don't use half of the ball — use the whole thing.

THE ULTIMATE LEAP OF FAITH

Perhaps the hardest thing in golf is to swing easily. That is, to hit the ball with your practice swing. If you're like most golfers, your practice swing is smooth and free flowing. When you take your practice swing, you focus on "the swing of it." When you take your actual swing, you focus on "the hit of it." Focusing on "the hit of it," you become what teaching pros call *ball conscious*. So how do you stop being ball conscious? By making the ultimate leap of faith.

Ponder this scenario. You're standing on the tee, loosening up to hit your drive. During your practice swings, you're feel oriented. You feel your relaxed grip, your soft forearms, your lively legs, your coiling hips and shoulders, your "long arms," your wide swing arc, and the clubhead swooshing through the air.

Suddenly, Al, your playing partner, who's standing by the ball washer, says, "Hey, look out behind you!" To your alarm, you see a mangy fox rushing toward you to bite you on the leg. (Don't laugh. I occasionally see foxes crossing the fairways on my course.)

Your only defense is your driver — a 10-degree, regular-flex, 460 cc, 42-inch TaylorMade club with an oversized grip.

Your driver happens to be your weapon of convenience. (Actually, you'd prefer a 5-iron, but there's no time to change clubs.)

As you prepare to defend yourself, would you entertain the same swing feelings as a moment ago? Would you try to relax your grip, soften your forearms, loosen your legs, coil your hips and shoulders, lengthen your arms, widen your swing arc, and swoosh the clubhead to increase clubhead speed?

I doubt it! If a rabid fox were about to bite you, you would have one overriding thought: KILL THE BASTARD! When you hit the panic button, your adrenaline starts flowing. You act instinctively. You resort to brute force. It's only natural. In fact, humans under duress have been wielding crude weapons and resorting to brute force since prehistory. So why should things be different when you're wielding a golf club?

This dramatic scenario illustrates why you become ball conscious. Let's consider why your actual swing — unlike your practice swing — tends to be tense and forced. The answer is obvious: your practice swing doesn't involve a ball (or a fox). There's no panic button, no performance anxiety, no adrenaline rush, no rapid breathing, no palpable stress, no survival mechanism, no dire consequences, no imminent threat, no do-or-die crisis, no lofty expectations. Other than that, the swings are identical!

Golfers, totally convinced that the ball won't go as far, rarely employ a swing that resembles their practice swing. The idea of a languid swing producing powerful results seems ridiculous and illogical. Even though Vijay, Ernie, and Freddie have easy, free-flowing swings that *do* produce power!

Psychologists use the term *counterintuitive* to denote an idea that seems the opposite of what you might suppose. Since such ideas seemingly defy logic, they are hard to accept. This is the case with the golf swing. But here's the reality of the situation: when you allow the clubhead to pick up its own speed — rather than forcing it with your hands — the clubhead actually moves faster. By tensing your hands to make the clubhead *go faster*, you actually slow it down.

Golf pros take a "look ma, no hands" approach. They generate immense power by languidly whipping the lagging clubhead through the air at its own speed. By relaxing your muscles and swinging more fluidly, you'll hit the ball farther. That's why a lot of petite women and scrawny kids can hit the ball so far.

You will hit the ball farther with a free-flowing swing because relaxed muscles move more quickly than tense muscles. The more relaxed your muscles, the more clubhead speed you will generate. And clubhead speed is a key variable in hitting the ball far.

Consider the times when you took an easy swing to subtract some yardage, only to find that you hit the ball farther than ever before. Swinging easily is counterintuitive but perfectly logical.

Try a simple experiment in relaxing your muscles and generating greater arm speed. Pretend you're a boxer. Try throwing punches with tense and rigid arms. You arms won't move very fast. Or pretend you're a baseball pitcher. Try throwing a ball with a tense and rigid arm. You won't be able to throw it very fast, especially if you grip the ball tightly in your fingers. Or try this: stand up and fully extend your arms out to the side. Compare *how quickly* your arms drop when they're limp with *how slowly* your arms drop when they're tense and forced.

Savvy boxers, pitchers, and golfers develop arm speed by relaxing their muscles. To make your arms and clubhead move faster, swing easier. Swing longer and more rhythmically by softening, relaxing, and lengthening your golf muscles, especially those in your arms. In the one-plane swing, you'll tend to use the lateral and rotational forces of your large muscles (legs, torso, and shoulders). In a two-plane swing, you'll tend to use your arms (not your hands) to whip the clubhead through the hitting zone.

My aim here is to awaken you to the basic actions, thoughts, and feelings associated with a free-flowing swing. Replace the impulse *to hit* with the impulse *to swing*. Swinging demands rhythm and timing. Hitting destroys rhythm and timing.

The more you try to speed up your swing, the more you'll tense up. Imagine your club making a big circle. Let "swoosh" become your simple pre-swing focus. Swing your long and short clubs with the same relaxed, languid tempo. Picture the swing of Ernie Els ("The Big Easy"). By relying more on images and feelings — and less on swing feelings and mechanics — you'll become less ball conscious. Begin by softening your muscles and swinging with only 85 percent of your power. Try it once!

All tour pros — despite unique differences in their swings, bodies, and personalities — share one thing: a free-flowing swing. To fulfill your golf potential you will have to make the ultimate leap of faith: to trust an easy, free-flowing swing to produce powerful results. As counterintuitive as it may seem, a free-flowing swing will elevate your game.

When a Native American shaman prepares young members of his tribe for their initiation ritual, he says:

> As you go the way of life,
> you will see a great chasm.
> Jump!
> It's not as wide as you think.

Making the ultimate leap of faith — to trust an easy, free-flowing swing — is one of golf's most important initiation rituals. If you wish to grow as a golfer, you must make the ultimate leap of faith. So jump!

METAPHOR

Sam Snead, playing on lightning-fast greens, composed a wonderful metaphor: "These greens are so fast," he said, "all I need to do is to hold my putter over the ball and hit it with my shadow." Conjuring the image of a shadow, Snead was able to send his muscles a clever message on how to execute a difficult putt.

Metaphors are figures of speech that compare two seemingly unrelated things. But metaphors are more than just figures of speech. They are ways of thinking. With them, golfers can organize, clarify, visualize, and learn complex and abstract concepts.

Lee Trevino used an interesting metaphor when he said that he wanted his lofted pitch shot "to land on the green like a mosquito with sore feet." Trevino provided himself with the perfect mental image to hit the shot exactly the way he wanted to. Creative visualization is an important part of learning the game. Golfers, like poets, cannot live without metaphors.

Many golfers use metaphoric visualizations to *simplify the complex*. To simplify the complex idea of hitting several inches behind a ball in a sand trap, Ray Floyd visualized the ball resting on a dollar bill. Eddie Merrins, "The Little Pro," used the image of swinging a club in a swimming pool to evoke among his pupils the feeling of swinging slowly.

In *The Seven Laws of the Golf Swing*, Nick Bradley uses imaginative visualization techniques to teach golfers the key aspects of the swing. The more striking the visualizations, the more memorable and useful they become.

I recommend two useful metaphors. First, to conceptualize the proper coiling of your torso, imagine your arms creating a three-dimensional hinging triangle swinging around the axis of your spine. Second, to conceptualize the baffling three-dimensional notion of the swing plane, imagine the angle your club shaft forms with the ground making an infinite number of parallel planes. Metaphors — conceptual tools — simplify the complex.

Visualization can also help you control your emotions. To replace anger with calmness, emulate Tibetan monks, who imagine a steady blue flame burning at their inner-center. They imagine the dancing and lambent flame becoming quiet and steady. When your emotions get the best of you, imagine that blue flame at your inner-center. It will return you there and restore your balance.

A quiet, steady, blue flame burning at your inner-center is only a metaphor. It acts as a momentary stay against confusion. So before you putt, inhale and imagine the inner flame. Visualize yourself absorbing inner light to illuminate awareness, clarity, and confidence. Feel the light relax you. Nerve tissue absorbs more light than do other tissues. Allow the light flowing outward and inward to give you mastery over your putts, your swing, your being.

LOOK AT THE BALL

Walter Travis, an expert putter, taught Bobby Jones how to "look" at the ball. Travis would visualize driving an imaginary tack into the back of the ball during the putting stroke. Since driving a tack is both a visual and tactile image, Jones learned to putt by combining look and feel.

Except in putting, you probably don't look at a particular spot on the ball. It's enough perhaps that you know precisely where your ball is. Looking is an act so familiar that you're not even conscious you're doing it.

However, your ball merits conscious looking. It's the object you're trying to strike. "You can't hit what you don't see!" is what my mentor used to say. During each shot, develop the habit of really looking at your ball.

In the East, students trained in meditation are taught to look at objects actively and alertly. This exercise — called "object meditation" or "one-pointedness" — is used by yogis and mystics to teach students how to focus. And focus is the axial skill in golf.

In object meditation, students select something to look at, perhaps a leaf or a rock. Next, they learn to look at the object as

if they were actually "feeling" it. They imagine its tactile qualities: texture, weight, temperature, contour. They practice uniting
sight and touch.

Try this simple exercise. Put a golf ball in your right hand.
Just look at it. Keep it still for one minute as you carefully examine it. Let your eyes gather in the ball. Next, close your eyes and
put the golf ball in your left hand. Feel it. Move it around for one
minute. Let your fingers and palm "learn" everything about the
ball. What is the difference between looking and feeling?

The difference is subtle, but quite important. Looking tends
to be nonverbal. You intuit what you feel. So what does this
mean to you as a golfer?

When you visualize, you translate your perceptions into
words that demand too much thinking. And thinking tends to
distract your attention or focus from where you need it most. But
when you "feel" the ball as you look at it, you clear your mind.
Feeling frees your mind of words and thought.

Each time you look at the ball, view it as a child would. Don't
verbalize or intellectualize your looking. Don't even think about
looking. When you realize that you're translating your looking
into words, go back to the nonverbal. Go back to feeling the ball
as you look at it. Feeling the ball with your eyes will quiet your
mind. Then merge *looking* and *feeling*. Practice object meditation to focus your mind.

So much in golf depends on the familiar act of looking. Miracles belong to golfers and monks who can perform one seemingly simple act: fixing their attention on only one thing at a time.
Golf doesn't require a lot of words or thinking. It requires attention. Don't verbalize. Don't intellectualize. Just work on being
totally present and totally alert.

IN THE ZONE

When you get in touch with your inner being, a special energy will flow inside you. You'll feel one with everything around you. It's what sports psychologists call "being in the zone." Being in the zone means becoming one with something large. Golf becomes large when you let go of reasoning, thinking, and conscious effort. You surrender to the spirit.

But what's the spirit? It's an energy field within you. It's an inner force that makes you grow. It's the great dynamic stillness where you can rest and relax. When you're in the zone, you'll glimpse the spirit of golf. You'll encounter something sublime both inside and outside yourself. You extend your boundaries and golf's boundaries. You no longer see yourself in the world of golf. You see the world of golf within you.

After years of success and failure you will hear the inner voice of the spirit. If you listen carefully and sensitively to it, you'll develop discernment. Without discernment you'll never enter the zone.

Discernment means listening carefully to yourself. For example, listen to your preshot questions: What club should I hit? How can I relax? How can I swing smoothly...stay focused

. . . follow through . . . make solid contact? The answers you seek do not flow from any prescribed set of laws or principles. The answers flow from discernment — from listening and surrendering. Only by listening openly and attentively to yourself can you become yourself.

Listening to your feelings is how to experience your body. By listening to your fear, tension, anxiety, or anger, you will discover your confidence, courage, contentment, and calmness. Listening lets you know what to let out and what to let in.

By listening, you can determine the direction of your golf thoughts. Suppose you and your partner are exactly 150 yards from the green. Your partner needs only an 8-iron. You, however, need a full 7-iron. So what do you do? If you ignore yourself and listen to your ego, you hit the 8-iron. Your ego won't let your partner outperform you. Naturally, you overswing and yank the ball hard left. Unfortunately, you listened to your ego, not to your inner voice.

Most of us are conditioned not to look inside. Maybe we're afraid of what we might see. To look inside is to confront your dark and shadowy realm. But it's your realm. If you don't look within, you'll never know what's inside you.

The zone is synonymous with peace of mind. To enter the zone is to revel in the sublime — in golf's magic. A chip-in for an eagle. A curling sixty-foot putt to save par. A birdie from a greenside bunker. A quiet stroll together up eighteen. Your love for golf isn't what matters. What matters is exhibiting and sharing that love. Golf has one heart and many heartbeats!

It's fine to understand golf's many theories, principles, and mechanics. It's fine to play at the highest level. It's fine to have the utmost confidence in your swing. It's fine to shoot a low number. These things are important. But these things don't represent the totality of golf. Unless you enter the zone, you'll remain a golfer with a small *g*.

CATERPILLARS AND BUTTERFLIES

When you walk your own path, you'll discover the mystery of golf. *Mystery* is not an adequate term. It would be best to use no name at all. Names set boundaries. The mystery of golf can never be explained or named.

Whether others take your same path is unimportant. Your business is to experience the mystery of golf for yourself. When you're ready, you'll find your own way up the mountain. You won't need guides or climbing aids to get you to the summit.

It's so easy in golf to become someone else without even knowing it. Your choices determine who you are. In life, your choices are the ground on which you stand. If you make choices to imitate or please someone else, someday you'll look in the mirror and sadly admit: "This isn't me. This isn't the person I'm supposed to be."

Golf speaks differently, sings differently, dances differently, resonates differently for each golfer. It offers each golfer a unique path. When the time comes, walk your own path. Otherwise you'll experience someone else's golf wisdom — never your own. Followers rigidly walk the path of others. Discoverers, however, walk their own path.

If you imitate, you're a golf follower, not a golf discoverer. You may imitate a golf legend like Ben Hogan or a phenom like Tiger Woods. But they're not you. They have a different body type, central nervous system, skill level, agenda, goal. You may follow the best golfer in the world without ever knowing why. You may always follow — reading the same articles, using the same driver, wearing the same hat as someone else. You may try to mimic the same swing and tempo of someone else, even though that swing and tempo do not speak to your nature.

But what's great about golf is its capacity to speak to everyone's unique nature. Golf lets you stand on your own two feet. To mimic implies looking outward. To discover implies looking inward. Eventually, you'll want to look within.

There's a curious South African caterpillar that plays a biological form of follow the leader. You might see hundreds of these creatures moving in a straight line. They follow the leader. Whatever the caterpillars ahead do, the next caterpillar does the same thing.

A biologist who studies these caterpillars tried an interesting experiment. On a circular, glass table top, he placed one caterpillar at the edge of the circle. Then he lined up the others, one behind the next, until the circle was complete. The caterpillars started to move around and around. They had no place to go but ahead and no place to rest. Remarkably, the caterpillars kept moving until they died of exhaustion. First the old ones died, then the young ones. After seven days, the glass table top was littered with dead caterpillars!

Golfers tend to imitate rather than discover. They follow the behavior, habits, and thinking of others. However, a caterpillar becomes a butterfly only when it goes inside the cocoon. Inside your "cocoon" is where you will experience the mystery of golf. Don't try to define or explain the transformative mystery. Just experience it! Become a butterfly, spread your colorful wings, and fly on your own.

PURE SEEING

Harvey Penick in his *Little Red Book* popularized the expression, "Take dead aim!" He said it was the most important advice in the whole book. The expression means that once you pick out your target, focus on it and nothing else. In the East, there's a similar and related concept called "pure seeing."

In golf you need to learn the habit of pure seeing. Playing the same golf course again and again, you tend to play it rotely. Seeing denotes serious viewing. Seeing, often taken for granted, takes practice. The two key obstacles to pure seeing are your *familiarity* and your *projections*.

You're too familiar with golf and the surroundings. Suppose you're hitting a wedge shot over a steep bunker guarding an elevated green. See the bunker as if you're seeing it for the first time, like a child. Otherwise you may hit your shot short and land in the bunker. Make the *familiar* into the *strange*.

The other obstacle is your projections. Projections are illusions. Seeing doesn't mean only seeing with your eyes. Pure seeing means stopping your projections — your illusions, viewpoints, fears, conditions. When your eyes stop imposing conditions on your golf shots, you can exercise pure seeing.

Suppose you're teeing off on a particularly tough par-4. This hole has eaten your lunch for years. There's water along the right side, pine trees on the left. To top it off, there's a fairway bunker two hundred yards out. You tense up. You no longer see the golf hole. What you see are your projections of the hole — your illusions and fears. Your eyes project only the difficulty ahead. You're convinced, from past experience, that a decent tee shot here is impossible. You're not *seeing*. You're *projecting*. When you project negative thoughts, your shots will follow.

Pure seeing is called "witnessing." So much of Eastern wisdom is implied in this term. Witnessing means watching yourself watching. It's the act of "watching the watcher." Witnessing involves simultaneously gazing *inside* and *outside*. To witness means uniting the watcher, the watched, and the watching.

Suppose you select a target somewhere on the course. As Penick said, you "take dead aim." You target a specific area on the fairway, or a spot on the green, or perhaps the cup itself. Once you select your target, exercise pure seeing. View it without any projections. See it unfiltered by fear or need. See it purely.

CLOUDS

Tibetan monks sit alone for hours observing clouds drifting by. They call it cloud meditation. Monks observe the clouds to access their composure. They observe, enter, then merge with the clouds. Their goal is to dissolve their egos and attachments. Sitting in a state of soft awareness, they celebrate the joy of the present moment. The monks, like the clouds themselves, are in no big rush.

When you walk the course, move like a cloud — especially if you are confused or upset. Forget your score or last poor shot. Just drift slowly. The tour pros do it. They move like clouds to access their inner calm. Quiet composure is like an open door. It allows harmony and rhythm and balance and peace of mind to enter. Without inner calmness, the doors are shut, and nothing meaningful can enter when you most need it.

If you stop to take a playing lesson from the clouds, you'll learn how to change directions in your swing. Instead of transitioning abruptly, tensely, and quickly from backswing to downswing, just imagine how a cloud would transition. Unlike golfers, clouds have no egos, agendas, or needs. They are totally patient and relaxed. When golf instructors tell you to change directions in your swing by "taking the air out of your arms," they're telling you to become "cloudlike." To change directions in your swing, don't force your arms downward. Simply let your soft and relaxed arms float down all by themselves.

Clouds are formless. They change from one moment to the next. And so does your golf game. One minute you're striking the ball solidly — the next you're hitting everything thin and off center. One minute you're drawing the ball — the next you're cutting it. One minute you're draining all your putts — the next you can't make a one-footer. Clouds and golfers are in constant flux. Their identity is defined by their impermanence.

Let's say that on the practice range you finally figure out how to hit your driver long and straight. Then you take your revelation to the course. Your so-called revelation, you discover, vanishes like a cloud. Most swing tips vanish like clouds.

You don't have to be a monk or go to the Himalayas to meditate on the clouds. Just walk under the open sky and look up. Make believe you have all the time in the world, like a cloud.

EFFORTLESS EFFORT

You can't play golf well if you expend too much energy or too little energy. You play well by expending the right amount of energy. In the East, there's an expression that applies directly to golfers: "Effortless effort."

Electricity moves between opposite poles. It's the only way it can move. Electricity needs both positive and negative poles. Your body also needs opposite poles to function properly. For example, your body during the golf swing bends like an archer's bow. Your body furnishes both flexibility and rigidity, stretch and resistance.

Your energy should flow like a river. A river has two opposing banks. When you use both banks — no matter how contradictory — your energy will flow naturally. Don't reject one bank and accept the other. If you identify with one thing too much, you'll lose your balance. You require both action and inaction, movement and stillness. You want your arms and shoulders, hips and legs to move. But you want your spine angle to remain fixed. You need both movement and stillness.

Don't play golf with too much right hand or too much left hand. Deep down they are one. Don't get stuck using one and not using the other. Both hands are yours. Golf energy flows evenly and naturally in both.

Try an experiment. Close your eyes and swing your 5-iron. You will discover that the distinction between left hand and right hand will disappear. You will learn to make your hands one. When energy flows equally in both hands, you will begin to swing rhythmically and naturally.

Finding the balance between opposites is the key to golf. Balancing opposites is essential to life as well. Don't judge or choose between opposites. Don't choose between doing and not-doing, thinking and not-thinking, effort and not-effort, fast and slow, right and left, loose and tight, noise and silence.

Rather, let your energy flow between the two poles. It's the most important thing you can learn about your golf swing. Letting your energy flow evenly between opposites is the way to achieve balance.

THE CENTIPEDE AND THE FOX

You might want to sit down. I have something very important to tell you: Swing thoughts don't work! In a swing lasting only 1.4 seconds, your brain can't handle all the millions of informational bytes involved. If you want to master the swing, drop swing thoughts.

It's like learning how to ride a bike. When you jump on your Schwinn, you don't employ "bike thoughts." You employ "bike feelings" to grasp that elusive combination of balancing, pedaling, and steering. Swing thoughts or bike thoughts are mechanistic. Swing feelings or bike feelings are intuitive. Swap thought for intuition. Use mechanistic thought to *discover* the proper swing. But use intuitive thought to *master* the proper swing.

Did you hear the tale about the centipede and the fox? It goes like this. A centipede was walking along on all one hundred legs, each leg perfectly in sync. No problems!

Then a fox came along. The fox, innately curious and logical about everything, carefully studied the centipede. He couldn't figure out how this creature could coordinate the movement of one hundred legs.

The fox asked, "How do you walk so smoothly and naturally?

I mean — how do you know which leg to move and when? Walking seems almost impossible!"

The centipede pondered the question and said, "Actually, I have been walking this way my whole life. I never even thought about it. But let me actually think about it for a minute."

So the centipede began to analyze his movement. He suddenly became both the *observer* and the *observed*. When he was just walking along, not thinking about his movement, he was one. Once he detached himself from his activity, he became two — subject and object. Suddenly, the centipede started to have serious locomotion problems. He fell over. He couldn't figure out how to coordinate all his legs.

Then the fox said, "Exactly! I knew it was hard to do. I'm surprised you could do it before."

Starting to weep, the centipede said, "Walking wasn't difficult before. But now you've created a big problem for me. I'll probably never be able to walk again."

When you analyze your swing, are you like the centipede? Do you try to analyze how your body can do a hundred different things at once? Do you analyze to the point of making the easy and the natural both complex and unnatural? If you have the mind of a fox, you'll ask questions, demand logic, intellectualize, and cripple your swing.

To understand your swing you need to *analyze* and *synthesize*. Analysis means breaking down your swing part by part. Synthesis means reassembling it part by part. Your intellectual faculties (logic and reason) are for analysis. Your emotional faculties (feeling and intuition) are for synthesis.

After you've learned the key club and body positions, let go of them. Just swing the club.

When you are whole, you are without impediment. "The man of Tao," said Chuang-Tzu, "acts without impediment."

THE ULTIMATE QUESTION

Golfers all ask the same questions: How can I hit it farther and straighter? How can I stop it — spin it — back it up? How can I work it right to left or left to right? How can I be more consistent? How can I swing and score like the pros? How can I slow down my swing? How can I beat Mario and get back some of the money I lost? These questions are all important. But none of these questions is the ultimate question: "Why do I play golf in the first place?"

In the East, Buddhist monks and nuns three times each day ask themselves, "Why was I born?" This question forces them to consider what they are doing. When monks ask themselves why they were born, the answer is always the same: "I am here to grow."

When you ask yourself, "Why do I play golf in the first place?" consider the same answer: "I play golf to grow." You may think that golf is all about scoring. If so, then golf is measurable and finite. If so, golf becomes a thankless obsession. If so, golf becomes a bottom-line issue like a bank account statement or a stock quote.

What happens when your score isn't good enough? Should

your scorecard determine whether you feel wonderful or not? If you want more from golf, don't define it only in terms of score.

You may not want to hear this, but you'll probably never be satisfied with the scores. You may spend decades striving for that ideal handicap, yet never achieve it. An acceptable score may be golf's ultimate illusion.

Decide whether you want to live with or without a score obsession. Decide whether score is so important that it trumps everything else, including your peace of mind. Given the choice between winning the U.S. Open next year and having perpetual peace of mind, which would you choose?

If you're making yourself miserable because you're not scoring, then move on. Frankly, it's not the score that's the problem. It's the tension over the score! The *I Ching*, the ancient book of Chinese wisdom, says that the events in your life are not what's important. What's important is how you respond to those events.

When you stress out over a poor score, your energy gets used up on tension. Energy isn't good or bad. It's just energy. Either it flows smoothly or it doesn't. When your energy gets stuck, you get tense. When it flows smoothly, you grow.

Your growth depends on how you use your energy. Growth simply means allowing your energy to flow smoothly. It comes with practice. It comes with surrendering to the scary uncertainty of your score.

If the joy of golf is reducible only to score, then golf is all about failure. Asking yourself, "When will my score will be good enough?" is like asking yourself when you'll be rich enough, healthy enough, or wise enough. Admit it — you'll *never* be rich enough, healthy enough, or wise enough! And your golf game will never be good enough. So don't let your score obsession stunt your overall growth. Make unconditional growth — golf and human growth — your main goal.

Don't misunderstand me. I'm not saying you should accept playing poorly. I'm just saying you should move beyond playing poorly. Don't make your happiness depend solely on score. Make your happiness depend on your peace of mind.

In 1923, according to an anonymous Internet piece, the president of the largest steel company was Charles Schwab, who died a pauper. The president of the largest gas company was Edward Hopson, who went insane. The president of the New York Stock Exchange was Richard Whitney, who was released from prison to die at home. The "Great Bear of Wall Street" was the nickname given to Cosabee Livermore, who eventually committed suicide. These barons of industry all died miserable.

That same year, the winner of the PGA Championship and the U.S. Open was Gene Sarazen. What happened to him? He golfed until he was ninety-two. He died contented and wealthy in 1999. The moral: Play golf! Be happy! Cultivate peace of mind!

Over ten centuries, Tibetan monks compiled sixty-four volumes of verse on the subject of inner growth. The main idea in all these books is a simple one. If you want to grow, relax. Stay in the moment. Be happy. And love your life.

Amen. That's today's sermon. Go in peace.

COMPOSURE

When you lose your dog or your cat, you immediately go and look for it. But when you lose your composure, what do you do? How do you find your composure?

To find your composure you need good thoughts to outweigh the frustration, anger, and self-doubt. You need an arsenal of affirmations to lift you up and get you back on track. Golfers especially need praise that is easily within reach.

Golf thoughts are like colored dyes. You can readily change the color of your thoughts. What you think in golf — or in life — is what you become. The ability to change your thoughts is your greatest power and mystery. In golf, your thoughts become your swing. And your swing becomes your shot. And your shots become your score.

Learn to dwell on those things that will improve, rather than perpetuate, your situation. Of the many choices you face in golf, the most important is attitude. Your attitude will decide your golf fate.

What dismays you is not the drive you snap into the woods or the short putt you miss. What dismays you is the way you distort and exaggerate these mishaps. On the course you can experience misery or bliss. The amount of energy and work involved in making yourself miserable or blissful is exactly the same.

Your thoughts contain the dyes that color your mind. If your mind is bathed in soft pastels, your swing is slow and effortless. If your mind is fiery red, your swing is fast and tense. The precursor of the golf shot is the golf thought.

When you take the driver out of your bag on the first tee, you immediately begin to color your thoughts. You *want* to put the ball in the fairway. You *want* your drive long and straight. You *want* to get off to a good start. You *want* to impress everyone watching. Your *wants* color your thoughts. Your mind is awash in red. You're swollen with need. However, what you really *want* is not a great drive. What you really *want* is the quiet composure to hit a great drive.

Don't fill your mind with red emotional dyes. If you do, you will grip the club too tightly and swing too quickly. Become aware of how you color your thoughts.

Watch where you put your eyes. Put your eyes where you want your emotions to go. Whatever you look at — the grip, the clubhead, the shaft, the fairway, the ball, the scorecard — tells your thoughts what emotional dyes you need for the swing to happen slowly and smoothly and effortlessly. Color your thoughts accordingly.

There is an Indian proverb that says everyone lives in a house with four rooms: the physical, mental, emotional, and spiritual. These are your four rooms in golf also. Live in all four rooms, not just the physical and mental. Dwell in all four, especially the emotional and spiritual rooms decorated in soft pastels to evoke composure.

CHECK YOUR BAGGAGE

Golf growth doesn't come easily. You have to work at it. The golf growth you get is the growth you create. Suppose you get a swing tip or a lesson from a savvy golfer. Do you know how to listen to that tip or lesson so you can benefit from it? If you don't know how to listen, how can you possibly improve? In fact, most golfers don't improve very much. They don't grow because they don't listen. They don't listen because they don't know how to listen.

If you listen with *fullness*, your mind is forever chattering inside. Your mind is jammed with mental traffic. It's too busy to listen. Your mind — like a plump sausage — is packed with golf knowledge. It's busy judging, evaluating, and thinking about what's right or wrong. Your mind is busy thinking about what fits and doesn't fit your present theory... about what's logical or illogical... about whether you really need this swing tip... about whether you want or need to change anything. Listening with fullness means you don't have the room or inclination to absorb anything.

If you listen with *emptiness*, however, your mind doesn't separate right from wrong. Nothing is right. Nothing is wrong.

There's nothing to evaluate — nothing to compare. Your mind is innocent and childlike. If you listen with emptiness, your mind disappears momentarily into the immediacy of the swing tip or lesson. Your mind is turned off. It's not running the show. It's completely open — free from judging, criticizing, believing, or disbelieving. You want only to understand and listen. After understanding occurs, you'll evaluate the swing tip or lesson. For now, you want only to remain open and available so growth can occur.

Listen to those who are golf worthy. And when you listen — just listen! Listen as if you were listening to a flute solo or a gurgling mountain stream. Listen without critically evaluating everything. Don't be a critic; be a listener. A critic makes room inside only to confirm what he already knows. A critic listens only if the swing tip or lesson fits what he already knows.

But what's already there is precisely the problem. Generally, what's already there isn't working. That's why you're getting a swing tip or lesson in the first place! Listening means that you "check your baggage" at the door. Check your baggage before you get your swing tip or lesson. Checking your baggage at the door means becoming empty. Otherwise, there's no room inside for any new and wonderful growth.

Suppose you're shopping at Wal-Mart. You buy two beach chairs, a large cooler, some underwear, and a large bottle of mouthwash. Next you go to Marshall's to get a new bathrobe. You decide to bring your previous purchases into Marshall's. (You just don't feel safe checking your stuff, so you carry around all your previous purchases.)

Suddenly, your shopping companion spots a flashy bathrobe she wants you to try on. You'd love to slip it on, but you can't. Your hands are full. It's too bothersome to set down all your stuff, just to try on a bathrobe! (Even though you went to Marshall's to buy a bathrobe in the first place.) So you leave, hauling around all the heavy stuff you got at Wal-Mart. Too bad — you missed out on a really nice bathrobe (on clearance, too!).

Having too much golf knowledge in your head is like carrying around so much stuff that you can't try on anything new. Being full means carrying around all your previous notions. Don't get me wrong. Listening with emptiness doesn't mean discarding your previous notions. It just means holding them in reserve to make room for new ideas about your game. Growth involves both subtracting and adding.

If you check your golf baggage at the front door, you can always pick it up on the way out. But unless you check your golf baggage, you'll never try on new stuff.

SETTLING YOUR MIND

ettle is what you say when your ball won't hold the green or the fairway. To settle means to cease all excess activity. Throughout your round, you constantly tell your ball to settle. However, it's even more important for your mind to settle down. Ultimate control in golf is in settling the mind — not the ball!

You settle your mind by emptying or deprogramming it. Emptying or deprogramming is Zen in a nutshell. Settling your mind means removing energy from your head. To do so allows you to play with penetrating awareness.

What are your typical preshot golf thoughts? Maybe your thoughts are cautionary reminders: Don't overswing! Don't swing fast! Don't hit the ball into the water on the right! Don't double-bogey this hole! Don't grip the club so tightly! Don't move your head! Don't drop your shoulder! Don't tense up!

When you first learned to drive a car, how many cautionary thoughts did your instructor give you? Whether you're driving a car or a golf ball, you need positive, clear, and simple thoughts. Cautionary or negative thoughts rarely help your body make a better swing. They're exactly the kind of help your body doesn't need. Before you swing, your body needs positive, clear, and simple energy.

Expect to settle your mind for only brief moments at a time. Your mind will shift constantly between unsettled and settled. You can't help that. When you feel tension, however, return to letting go. Tension is caused by clinging. Clinging means thinking too much about the past or the future. It means thinking about your swing, your score, your ego. Letting go is the only path to greater inner peace and awareness. In the East they say, "An active mind is sick. A settled mind is healthy. And a still mind is divine."

An unsettled mind is like the restless and grasping trunk of an elephant. It grabs everything in sight. During crowded festival days in India, elephants are a big nuisance. Their trunks snatch bananas, trinkets, blankets, and anything colorful. To settle them down, their handlers place a bamboo stick in their trunks. The stick occupies their trunks and settles them down. So too with you. You need something to occupy your mind.

There are three good ways to settle the mind: by following your breathing, by repeating certain vibrational sounds or chants (mantras), and by visualizing. All three remove excess energy from your head. They will help you stop clinging to thoughts.

Breathing exercises will settle your mind and body. Shift your conscious attention to your breathing and away from everything else. Sense your breaths passing in and out of your nostrils. Count every exhale in sets of five or ten. Breathe rhythmically, calmly, and naturally. With every inhale, liberate all unneeded energy and tension. Let go of your thoughts. Return to your breathing.

Chanting exercises use sound energy to settle your mind. This is a mantra technique. Silently repeat again and again a phrase of affirmation. It doesn't matter what phrase you use. Chant, "I am one with my body." Chanting the mantra will empty your mind and create a sense of dynamic stillness. Your mind and body will become wonderfully serene. Your mind will suddenly become clear and rested.

Visualization exercises use calming mental pictures to settle your mind. Monks, for example, form indelible images of still candle flames, reflective ponds, and melting blocks of ice. Visualize and embrace the serenity of these images. Use these and other images to dissipate your tension.

When your ball settles on the fairway or on the green, that's great. But when your mind settles on the fairway or the green, that's even greater.

DEEP LONGING

After sixteen agonizing holes, you get a flash of intuition. You realize that your swing plane has been too flat, or your posture has been too stooped over, or your ball position has been too far back. So for the last two holes, your game is on fire. You're convinced you've just found the last piece of the puzzle. You're miffed that you must wait a whole week before you can play again. Inside you yearn to hit another drive or crush another 6-iron. Inside you is deep longing.

Edward Gibbon, the noted historian, devoted his adult life to a literary project of major proportions. He spent thirty-three years writing *The Decline and Fall of the Roman Empire*. He worked with relish on his project every day for thirty-three years. Biographers claim Gibbon never aged during that span. When he was fifty years old, he completed his project. The day he finished the book, he actually cried. Working on his book, he felt so rich. Completing his masterpiece, however, he felt so poor. His wife couldn't understand his reaction. His wife wanted to celebrate his achievement to cheer him up. But Gibbon refused: "My work is complete. What's left for me? My life is over." Seven years later, he died an old man at fifty-seven!

Luckily, your golf game will never be finished. It will always remain under construction. Every golf game will fall short. Inherent in every round is the pure longing to try again tomorrow. And when tomorrow comes and goes, the longing will remain. Never expect to be happy or contented with your game. Just keep on playing and keep on longing. "It's the intensity of the longing," Kabir wrote, "that does all the work."

All golfers have both ambitions and longings. The two are quite different. Ambitions are goal based. Longings are source based. Ambitions are specific thoughts that reside in your head. Longings are general feelings that reside in your heart. Ambitions involve external things — low scores, trophies, long drives — that you hope to achieve. Longings involve internal things — heartfelt yearnings to reach the unattainable. You can never fulfill a longing. Longings exist only for their own sake. To become a total golfer, entertain both ambitions and longings.

Recently, a friend and I viewed a special exhibit of Vincent van Gogh's paintings at the Metropolitan Museum of Art. There I saw the actual painting of a print that hangs in my office. This particular painting, like so many of Van Gogh's works, features giant trees that reach to the stars. My friend, an art buff, explained that Van Gogh's enormous trees express the artist's earthly longings to reach for the heavens. Simply put, Van Gogh wasn't painting *trees* — he was painting *longing*!

And so too with you. Your earthly golf longings are like the trees touching the stars in Van Gogh's paintings. Whether Van Gogh's trees or your golf longings are realistic doesn't mean diddly-squat. What matters is that you keep reaching for the stars. What matters is that you appreciate longing for the sake of longing. What matters is that you fill your heart with longing.

When your longing ends, golf will end. The Buddhist word *nirvana* means "to blow out" or "extinguish." Is that what you really want — to blow out your golf candle and attain nirvana? Or would you prefer to keep your golf candle burning to kindle the joy of deep longing? Be careful what you wish for. Deep longing is what it feels like to feel really good. Deep longing, Dear Golfer, is what living a golf-intoxicated life is all about!

YOUR SHADOW

In golf, your personal qualities, expectations, and physical skills follow you like a shadow throughout your days. Your golf shadow — your double — rides on your shoulders, watching every shot, mimicking every gesture, and walking every step of your path. Your shadow is a total reflection of you. The Buddha once said, "All that you are is the result of what you have thought. If you speak or act with an evil thought, pain follows you. If you speak or act with pure thought, happiness follows you like a shadow that never leaves you."

Whether you're comfortable or uncomfortable with your shadow depends on how fulfilled you are. You may enjoy golf success like trophies and championships. But success is worthless if it doesn't fulfill you. Life is ultimately about fulfillment, not success. If you're unfulfilled, your shadow will haunt you.

Legendary golfers have cast long and indelible shadows over the game. The greatest golfers are remembered as much for their personal qualities as for their championships. Almost every golf course bears the lengthened shadow — the sacred aura — of one particular and special golfer. Over Augusta National and Pinehurst, for example, hang the imposing shadows of Bobby Jones and Sam Snead, respectively. Their days have sped by, but not their shadows. All golfers walk in the giant shadows of Jones, Snead, and other great champions. Golfers are shadow walkers.

There's nothing demeaning about walking in someone's shadow. Even Jack Nicklaus is a shadow walker. His first (and perhaps only) golf hero was Jones. Nicklaus, having walked in Jones's shadow, has become a great champion in his own right. Had Nicklaus not walked in Jones's shadow, he might not have assumed the exemplary modesty and grace of his hero. For decades to come, golfers will walk in the shadows of Nancy Lopez, Annika Sörenstam, Tiger Woods, Ernie Els, Vijay Singh, and other greats.

However, Augusta National and Pinehurst are not the only courses with imposing shadows. Go to any small golf course and read the names etched on the plaques and trophies in the clubhouse. Those are the names of cherished local golfers whose spirits still abide and shadows still remain. Their achievements and personal qualities still hang in the air.

One October I stumbled on a quaint, nine-hole, family-owned golf course in a western Massachusetts hill town deep in the Berkshires. An ancient potbellied stove heated the old clubhouse. From the dusty plaques on the wall, I read the names of club champions dating back to the 1930s. At that moment I glimpsed the shadows of golf ghosts, their faded glory mingling with the wood smoke of a late autumn afternoon.

Your shadow is but a projected image of yourself. When your body intercepts light rays cast on a surface, your shadow appears. In kindergarten, perhaps your teacher made a silhouette of you as a keepsake. Shining a large incandescent lamp on your head, your teacher projected your portrait onto a screen. Then your teacher cut out your profile on black paper and pasted it on a white backdrop. A silhouette is a well-defined shadow. In many ways golf, too, shines a light that projects a well-defined profile on a large screen for all to see.

When golf shines directly on you, your profile instantly appears. When golf projects your image on a public screen, it reflects everything about you, inside and out. Your golf silhouette is made up of a thousand meticulous details, especially in the etiquette you observe.

For example, the way you mark your ball... keep still and silent when others are swinging... fix your divots... keep "the sacred the area around the hole"... leave the rake outside the trap ...tend the flagstick...stand to the side when others putt...wait your turn to play...drive your cart in the fairway.

Or...the way you step over the intended putting line of others...leave the green as soon as the last putt clicks in the cup...quietly lay down your golf bag...mercifully pick up your ball (in a nontournament) during a double-digit hole...turn off your cell phone...quietly crunch your corn chips...refrain from jingling the loose change in your pocket...shake hands after you lose.

When golf's light shines on you, it also captures your adherence to the game's time-honored rules. The rules of golf, seemingly a cold piece of business, are the game's great equalizer. What applies to you, for example, playing a friendly match on your local golf course applies to Tiger Woods playing in the Masters. The rules of golf boil down to several basic ethical principles: play your own ball as it lies and play the course as you find it. These ironclad principles — as well as the game's official rules — create a tidy, moral framework for golf. What makes golf special, unlike other sports, is that its rules are self-enforced. The nobility of golf flows from its ability to bring out the very best in people.

However, we all know golfers who cast a long and vulgar

shadow over the sacred principles of the game. How you play the game is essentially how you live your life in general. The little things in life make up the big things. When golfers violate the principles of the game, the only thing they lose is their self-respect. When golfers lose their self-respect, they cast a large and inescapable public shadow. Your golf shadow is a projection of many things, including your ability, conduct, and character.

When golfers violate the rules, they become casualties of their own lofty expectations. Some expectations are imposed from inside, others from outside. When golfers with high expectations and strong obsessions choose to gain an advantage by improving their lie rather than play the ball exactly as it is, they are no longer in charge. Their expectations are in charge! Your golf shadow will disturb you if you let your expectations run the show. Shadows are like families or roommates — you have to live with them.

A parable by Chuang-Tzu deals with a man who runs away from his shadow. The man, made constantly miserable by the sight of his shadow, resolves to lose it. He decides to run away from it once and for all. With every step, however, the shadow stays close behind him. The man runs even faster. Faster and faster he runs. He doesn't stop running until he drops dead in his tracks. Then Chuang-Tzu ends the parable by saying something really interesting: the man never realized that he needed only a spot of shade to make his shadow vanish.

The "shade" that Chuang-Tzu is referring to here is your inner stillness and peace of mind. The sun's rays can't enter your shade — your inner being. Your shade is a quiet and empty state of pure being. When you retreat to your private shade, your publicly projected shadow will vanish. Perhaps the man in the parable wanted to escape his disturbing shadow because it showed his ambition, greed, or fear. But ambition, greed, and fear are part of society. Ambition, greed, and fear don't exist without society. When you withdraw to your inner quiet, ambition, greed, and fear vanish like a shadow in the shade. The parable is about going within to find your shade.

When your shadow walks beside you on the fairway, cherish it as your truest and oldest golf companion. It's been there faithfully during good rounds and bad. It was there the day, in fact, you fired your lowest round and won some money from both your boss and your district manager! (You won't soon be forgetting the looks on their faces when you took their money.)

It was there the day before you got married when nearly your whole wedding party played golf, and everyone (even the women) smoked cigars. It was there the day you finally realized your posture was too bent over because you actually paid attention to what your shadow was telling you.

Your golf shadow goes way back with you. Moreover, your shadow may continue long after you're gone. Decades from now in a rustic clubhouse, golfers may also catch a glimpse of your shadow mingling with the wood smoke of a late autumn afternoon.

AFTERWORD

by Thomas Moore

There is more to a game than meets the eye. Nongolfers sometimes ask, What drives grown men and women to hit a little ball, chase it, and go into tantrums if they don't hit it into a hole in the ground? I suspect that the meaning of life might be hidden in the answer to that question. Like any sport, golf is a ritual that sums up the tensions and dynamics of life. A golf course is a universe in miniature, and a round of golf a symbolic circling of the challenges you encounter in the eighteen holes of your life.

Centuries ago, poets described the game of billiards in similar fashion. They said that the green felt of the pool table symbolizes the field on which life plays itself out. The holes in the table were called hazards, just like obstacles in golf. The number eighteen is also significant. Early philosophers interested in game theory and play, known as Neoplatonists today, thought most highly of the number nine. It is thrice three, the number of perfection. It is also just shy of ten, the number indicating a complete set. In other words, golf is never over, and the golfer is always one shot or one hole or one game short of perfection.

James Ragonnet understands that a game of golf always points beyond itself. To play it well you have to have qualities of character that, oddly, are the same required to be a spiritual master. Maybe golf, then, is a spiritual exercise, a way to learn how to be and live, and not just how to spend an afternoon.

This book contains many lessons on how to approach golf as a centered, focused, settled human being. This book is about how to use golf to help you develop such mastery in life. You don't want to take the fun out of the game, but you might use the game for greater profit. This book has some wisdom for you that will help both your game and your life. What more could you ask for?

Gnosticism, a spiritual movement popular around the time of Jesus Christ, taught that in its descent into human life the soul passes through seven planetary spheres, or archons, where it encounters the special spirit of each. I imagine golf as a similar movement of soul: each hole has its own demands, each with its own terrain and planetary quality. You have to survey each and understand its particular challenge. At the end of each hole you score yourself: How well did I do with this particular challenge? What unexpected obstacles did it present? How will I deal with it next time?

I have long believed that every person is capable of becoming an "ordinary mystic." By that I mean we can all become contemplative in simple ways, deepening the place from which we live and finding spiritual meaning where we didn't think it existed. I've learned from this book that golf is a good path to this everyday mysticism. The game is a ritual, a meditation, and a symbolic journey.

The next time you play golf, remember that a round of golf is a practice run around life's opportunities and hazards. Enjoy the game, but not unconsciously. Know that it is a school for the soul, a way to recall and learn how to deal with life's hazards and traps, bunkers and roughs. You can learn, in the face of life's unpredictability, how to stand, grip, and swing. You can prepare yourself for whatever challenges the next archon in your life has in store for you.

ACKNOWLEDGMENTS

To any reader who's considering writing a book connecting golf to Eastern spiritual precepts and practices, I strongly advise you to do what I did:

Work in a nurturing environment — like that of Springfield College in Springfield, Massachusetts — that will generously award you a precious sabbatical so you can think, research, and write.

Seek the guidance of a brilliant and compassionate Buddhist scholar, mentor, and friend — like Taitetsu Unno, former Jill Ker Conway Professor of Religion at Smith College — to dazzle and awaken you.

Receive the inspiration and encouragement of a sage, friend, and bestselling author — like Thomas Moore — who will lend his support and teach you to look anew at reality.

Stumble on an enlightened golf guru and friend — like John Cipollini — to help you probe and understand the hidden intricacies and nuances of the golf swing.

Secure a supportive, tireless, and savvy literary agent — like Jacques "The Shankster" de Spoelberch — to steer you in the right direction and to fuel your tank when you're running on empty.

Partner up with a talented, insightful, and congenial editorial team — like my editor, Jason Gardner, at New World Library, managing editor Kristen Cashman, and copyeditor Paula Dragosh — whose sharp red pencils will tighten, cut, and improve your manuscript beyond belief. ("If you guys can clean up this manuscript," I told them, "then there's still hope for Lake Erie!")

Then mention that there are far more people — like my loved ones, friends, playing partners, colleagues, and students — than you can possibly thank for your book's evolution. With your palms together, bow to them all. And pray they realize that your collective reference to their fellowship and encouragement, nonetheless, conveys the full measure of your gratitude.

If I were you, that's exactly what I would do.

ABOUT THE AUTHOR

James Ragonnet, PhD, is an award-winning English professor at Springfield College in Springfield, Massachusetts. For three decades he has exhaustively analyzed and researched golf to discover and master what works, what doesn't, and why. He also has a consulting firm that targets corporate executives and college faculty interested in enhancing their teaching, learning, and writing. Whether he's focusing on better golfing, better writing, or better teaching, Ragonnet's specialty is developing effective learning strategies for complex tasks. He has also taught and coached college golf. His website is www.golfsthreenobletruths.com.

NEW WORLD LIBRARY is dedicated to publishing books and other media that inspire and challenge us to improve the quality of our lives and the world.

We are a socially and environmentally aware company, and we make every attempt to embody the ideals presented in our publications. We recognize that we have an ethical responsibility to our customers, our employees, and our planet.

We serve our customers by creating the finest publications possible on personal growth, creativity, spirituality, wellness, and other areas of emerging importance. We serve our employees with generous benefits, significant profit sharing, and constant encouragement to pursue the most expansive dreams. As a member of the Green Press Initiative, we print an increasing number of books with soy-based ink on 100 percent postconsumer waste recycled paper. Also, we power our offices with solar energy and contribute to nonprofit organizations working to make the world a better place for us all.

Our products are available
in bookstores everywhere.
For our catalog, please contact:

New World Library
14 Pamaron Way
Novato, California 94949

Phone: 415-884-2100 or 800-972-6657
Catalog requests: Ext. 50
Orders: Ext. 52
Fax: 415-884-2199
Email: escort@newworldlibrary.com

To subscribe to our electronic newsletter, visit
www.newworldlibrary.com